**This book is to be returned on or before
the last date stamped below.**

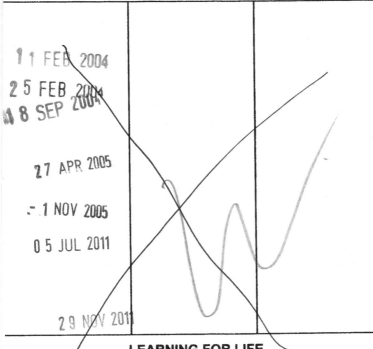

1 1 FEB 2004

2 5 FEB 2004

1 8 SEP 2004

2 7 APR 2005

- 1 NOV 2005

0 5 JUL 2011

2 9 NOV 2011

**LEARNING FOR LIFE
LONDON BOROUGH OF SUTTON LIBRARIES**

RENEWALS   Please quote: date of return, your ticket number
and computer label number for each item.

Practical books that inspire

How to Make Money from Property
The expert guide to property investment

Making Money from Letting
How to buy and let residential property for rent

But Your Home at Half the Price
*A step-by-step guide to reducing the price of a house and cost
of your mortgage*

Managing Your Personal Finances
How to achieve your own financial security, wealth and independence

howtobooks

Pleae send for a free copy of the latest catalogue to:

How To Books
3 Newtec Place, Magdalen Road
Oxford OX4 1RE, United Kingdom
Tel: (01865) 793806   Fax: (01865) 248780
email: info@howtobooks.co.uk
http://www.howtobooks.co.uk

Save £1000s Selling Your Own Home

*Learn an estate agent's secrets
and make more money selling
your house yourself*

TONY BOOTH

howtobooks

First published by How To Books Ltd,
3 Newtec Place, Magdalen Road,
Oxford OX4 1RE, United Kingdom.
Tel: (01865) 793806. Fax: (01865) 248780.
email: info@howtobooks.co.uk
http://www.howtobooks.co.uk

British Library Cataloguing in Publication Data.
A catalogue record for this book is available from
the British Library.

Cover design by Baseline Arts Ltd, Oxford

Produced for How To Books by Deer Park Productions
Edited by Diana Brueton
Typeset by Kestrel Data, Exeter
Printed and bound by Cromwell Press Ltd, Trowbridge, Wiltshire

NOTE: The material contained in this book is set out in good
faith for general guidance and no liability can be accepted
for loss or expense incurred as a result of relying in particular
circumstances on statements made in the book. Laws and
regulations are complex and liable to change, and readers should
check the current position with the relevant authorities before
making personal arrangements.

Contents

Acknowledgements

To my partner Rik Perkin for the support and encouragement given and for enduring the long periods of research, writing and clicking from the keyboard that went into the making of this book. To my good friend Alan Lancaster for proofreading and for giving consistently sound and constructive advice. To solicitor Mat Slade of Fidler and Pepper (solicitors) whose guidance and suggestions have been invaluable and whose contribution has helped formulate a more precise legal reference. To Nikki Read and all at How To Books for their support and assistance and for providing me with the opportunity for publication. And finally to my late parents, Dorothy and Gerald, who encouraged me to write from an early age and whose qualities of perseverance and determination have been inspirational throughout my life.

Preface

Despite the myth, bubbling fresh coffee in the kitchen and a warm glow from an open fire are not going to be enough to sell your property. It will take a good deal more than this to entice the home-hunter to part with his money. The recipe for a successful sale involves a little planning and a moderate amount of effort blended with a pinch of good fortune. When combined with the secret ingredient – an estate agent's inside know-how – the results can be astounding! It will also save you thousands of pounds in professional fees.

This book will guide you through each stage along the road to selling your property. It will help you to understand the various procedures involved and provide you with the rare opportunity of actually sitting in the driver's seat. So often vendors complain of feeling as though they are no more than a passenger with the agent steering. They feel insecure and cautious, not quite knowing what is going on around them and not entirely certain of the direction they are heading. This book will get you directly involved in your own destiny. *You* will be selling your home. *You* will receive interested viewers and 'make the deal'. *You* will be in charge. By reading just a few pages you will realise you *can*:

- cut out the middle-man

- keep the commission fee in your own pocket

- and sell your property faster and for a higher value.

There are secrets and tricks that make life easier in just about every trade and profession known to the modern world, and estate agency is no different. It often surprises me to find that so few people actually take the plunge to sell their property themselves. It is said that there is a salesman in all of us – we are after all a nation of shopkeepers – yet we hand over the sale of what is financially our greatest asset in life to a person for whom we have only contempt and we then pay them for the privilege!

Selling property is not rocket science – though some agents would have you believe otherwise. It is rather more like an involved game of chess . . . you know the end is coming but you can never be quite certain of when until the last few moves are played. The game involves suspense, competition and communication. There can be a frenzy of activity one minute, followed by a steady and slightly unnerving tranquillity the next. First one side seems to have all the pieces stacked in its favour then the other side gains a little ground and takes control. During this game I intend you to finish as the winner, having had a thoroughly enjoyable time in the process.

Imagine that . . . **selling your home and enjoying it!**

Some people may be daunted by the legalities of selling a property and, given the complexity of the law, this is quite understandable. Bear in mind that you will be leaving much of the legal aspects of the sale to your appointed solicitor or conveyancing agent. You will not – and frankly should not – attempt to deal with matters of contract law. This is one area best left to the professionals. There are however some parts of the legal arena you can enter, if you so wish, and this book will guide you safely through those areas. This will result in reduced legal fees and, more importantly, a considerable saving of time. Acting for yourself rather than entirely depending on your solicitor can subtract up to four weeks from the normal period it takes to reach exchange of contracts.

The parts of this book that refer to legal aspects are only applicable to those selling property in England and Wales. Other countries have different laws and legal procedures and you must always seek advice from solicitors familiar with the pertinent laws of the country in which you are selling. The remaining elements of this book refer to the preparation of your property for sale and how to seek and secure a buyer – these aspects are the same the world over and there are estate-agency secrets disclosed herein that will bring you closer to your objective.

You will need to be highly motivated to find your buyer and this book will ensure you keep to the right track by offering guidance and encouragement. You will quickly discover that there are numerous advantages to learning your new skills. Not only will you save thousands of pounds but you will also:

- Gain a unique hands-on insight into how the property market operates from an estate-agent's perspective.

- Understand how to deal with solicitors and their enquiries.

- Learn how to sell effectively and attract the highest offers.

- Discover how to improve the appearance of a property cheaply and easily.

- Master the art of communicating constructively with a wide variety of people.

These skills can then be applied and utilised repeatedly throughout your life when buying or selling any other property. Even if in the future you decide to employ the services of an estate agent rather than going it alone, the levels of competence you will achieve through this book will provide you with the wisdom and experience needed to understand what the agent *should* be undertaking on your behalf.

So, step on board . . . and let's get moving!

Tony Booth
e-mail: tonybooth@quays.demon.co.uk

1

The Best Time to Sell

The age-old concept of supply and demand is worth considering long before you erect a 'for sale' sign. Even though your product (the property) may not be fully prepared to enter the market – it *is* available – and can therefore be *supplied*. But is there enough *demand* to attract a high volume of viewers? Much will depend on the time of year.

THE MOST LUCRATIVE MONTHS FOR SELLING

The hottest months

The sale of residential property generally follows seasonal rules, with minor fluctuations influenced by the country's economic performance and in particular whether interest rates are high or low. Interest rates only control the market by turning the volume up or down but rarely impede forward momentum. This makes the market relatively predictable month to month and year on year. There are exceptions, notably during severe recession, but fiscal changes introduced by government after the last housing crisis are likely to prevent any future dramatic downturn or another nationally experienced bricks and mortar equity disaster.

> **Estate agent's secret**
> Some agents will tell you that it is never the wrong time to sell. This is not true. Timing is everything. Selling at the right time of the year can result in high viewing numbers and preferred offers.

April and May are always the hottest months for selling property. People have spent the cold winter months considering their options and planning for the year ahead. Once Christmas and New Year are truly over, and the sun starts to shine, buyers go out in an abundance searching for their new home. The spring-season inspires and motivates people. It nurtures confidence and encourages the house-hunter to actively pursue their goal.

Spring also brings out first-time buyers and these are an enormously important group in the housing market. They provide fuel in the form of finance so that others further up the ladder can move. During these two energetic months housing chains can rattle along at a frantic pace. If you can place your property on the market during early April there is every chance it will have sold by the end of May, and at the asking price or even more if there is poor local competition.

The warmest months

June, July and August are good for selling though slower than April and May. This is a period when people tend to have other things on their minds. They are likely to be planning for and looking forward to a summer holiday, having day trips, taking care of children during the summer break, redesigning their garden or simply enjoying weekend barbecues in it with their family and friends.

Whilst this period produces long spells of good hot weather during which you may think people would want to view properties, the fact is, that there are often just not enough hours in the day for them to concentrate on this aspect of their lives. Those who have got the time, however, will want to secure a property before winter sets in.

The coolest months

September, October, November and March are quiet months in the property market. As the cold weather begins people start to batten down the hatches for winter. The desire to leave their own cosy home to look at others diminishes and by November their minds turn to preparations for the festive season. The buyers who are looking for property at this time are aware that owners may be under pressure to sell and will generally make low offers in the hope of getting a bargain.

March can either be a cool or a warm month for selling and this literally depends on the weather. If it is wet and cold then viewings are likely to be few and far between. On the other hand if it is dry, and preferably sunny too, then potential buyers will be keen to view the first properties entering the market early in the season.

The frozen months

December, January and February are the most dubious months of the year for selling property. It is generally very cold, very wet, and during December people are absorbed in their plans for Christmas and the New Year. By mid-January most people are exhausted after entertaining friends and relatives, they may be returning from a festive holiday or getting back into the work routine. Others will simply be hibernating and waiting for the warmer weather before venturing out.

The only buyers available for viewings will be those desperate to secure a property quickly. It may be that their own home has sold and they need to find somewhere else to live to ensure their own sale does not collapse. Or they may find themselves suddenly in need of more space, for example where an addition to the family is expected. In any event such buyers will be scarce and most properties can expect perhaps only one or two viewings each month, if any at all.

Indirectly what may seem a hopeless situation can work to your advantage. Desperate buyers will often pay the asking-price for a property they like and will be keen to secure it as quickly as possible. Though such opportunities may be thin on the ground there is always good reason to be optimistic about a viewing arranged, even during the worst months of the year.

USING THE QUIET SEASON TO PLAN A STRATEGY

Take advantage of the quiet months. The winter period is an ideal time, whilst the market is quiet, for you to plan your selling strategy. Your preparations should include:

- A target date for erecting your 'for sale' sign.

- Taking care of improvements to your property including any redecoration that may be required.

- Researching the neighbourhood and gathering essential data and statistics.

- Obtaining brochures from estate agents of properties for sale nearby.

- Inviting estate agents to your home to give a free and no-obligation value opinion and extracting from them any useful information on how the local property market is performing.

- Asking friends and relatives to act as critical (but constructive) potential buyers, enabling you to identify problem areas that might be remedied before the property is introduced to the market.

- Having a good clear-out of all clutter and giving your property a thorough, early spring clean.

LEARNING TO THINK LIKE A SALESMAN

Selling is an art and some are better at it than others, but it is a skill anyone can learn and many already practise these abilities subconsciously in their everyday lives. Think about the last time you sold something to someone else and identify what you did to achieve it. Have you ever sold a car or an item of furnishing? Do you sell your services as part of your job? Are you self-employed? Have you ever had to sell an idea to improve your company's trading figures or promote a new management scheme?

Consider all of these experiences as learning

opportunities. If something you did worked well then recognise it and adapt it for use when selling your home. It is equally important to acknowledge what may not have worked well to ensure that such mistakes are not repeated.

An estate agent is an unbiased salesman who will offer your property for sale by promoting its best features to the general public. To succeed, you must do the same. But you have lived in it, decorated it, cared for it and protected it, and as a result you are likely to have an emotional attachment to it. Whilst it may be difficult to detach yourself from the property you call home this will be essential if you are to sell it effectively. To this end begin looking at your house or apartment as a commodity, a product with a price-tag stuck to it, something that will eventually realise capital allowing you to move on to better things. Keep this thought in mind and you will gradually withdraw from any emotional connection and become a better salesman as a result.

PICKING THE BEST TIME FOR YOU

To sell your property successfully you must:

- Be 100% committed to selling it.

- Be fully prepared for the throng of viewers touring through your home who will inspect every crevice and cupboard.

- Have the energy and stamina to withstand constant viewings and the preparation required for each one.

- Be virtually free from any other stressful events happening in your life that may otherwise distract or influence you, such as a pregnancy, school holidays, an impending close family wedding, an ongoing illness, problems or pressures in your career, a driving test or higher-education exam, or financial problems.

- Have the full support of your partner (if appropriate) and be able to rely on a close friend or family member if the going gets tough.

- Believe in yourself so that others will believe in you.

If the time is not right for you to sell don't attempt it. Wait until personal and career pressures have subsided and you are in good health. Trying to get the time of the year favourable and your own personal situation at its best may be quite a juggling act and a compromise will likely have to be established. Realise that the more compliant your situation, the more promising the outcome will be. By creating the best circumstances in which to achieve the sale of your property you will be able to take advantage of the opportunities generated.

KEEPING AN EYE ON LOCAL INFLUENCES

Study your neighbours and the neighbourhood! Bear in mind that prospective buyers will not only wish to inspect the property of their dreams but will also have aspirations and expectations about the area in which they wish to live. Many of us are so familiar with the locality that we tend to look at it through blinkered eyes. Some may not have walked around the neighbourhood for years and as a result will know little about changes that have occurred, but newcomers to the area will survey everything and will register the good and bad aspects of it.

There are a variety of reasons why you should start examining your neighbourhood at the earliest opportunity. These include:

- To gather information and data on any nearby properties up for sale and assess the reasons why particular properties appear to sell faster than others.

- To collect the prices of similar properties to your own that are for sale and judge whether values are on their way up or on their way down.

- Contacting the local authority planning department and obtaining or getting on a mailing-list to receive details of planning applications as they are submitted.

- Identifying potential obstacles to selling your property, such as a bus-stop or signpost immediately outside your home. Consider complaining about it to the local authority or transport department and propose that it is moved or improved.

- Objecting to any planning application you feel will affect the value or charm of your property and rallying neighbours to do the same.

- Writing letters to the local authority to ensure graffiti is removed from any walls or buildings, trees are pruned, grassed borders on the public highway are cut and properly maintained, repairs to the roads and pavements are undertaken, litter is picked up, broken road-signs are replaced and street lights all operate properly.

- Joining a residents' association and encouraging action by it to improve the neighbourhood. If there is no residents' association – consider creating one.

TO SUMMARISE

- Plan to launch your property on the market for sale during April to attract the greatest number of potential buyers and acquire the highest possible offers.

- Use the winter period to prepare yourself and your property for selling.

- Realise that your home is merely a saleable product made up of bricks and mortar. Reduce the emotional attachment you have for it by recognising the capital value it holds and associate that value with your future plans.

- Be certain that your personal circumstances are compatible with the stresses involved in selling your home.

- Examine your neighbourhood and assess ways in which it might be improved.

- Identify other properties for sale in the locality and gather information on them, including the asking price.

2

How to Create *the* Des Res

The desirable residence is what most buyers are looking for and your task will be to transform your investment into a property that meets the aspirations of the majority. You must forget the idea that your house is *your* home – it now needs to be turned into *everyone else's* home – thereby making it attractive to the greatest number of people.

Obstacles to overcome are familiarity and identity. Like all home-owners you are likely to have stamped on the property your own individuality and personal preferences. Colours and furnishings will be those of your own choosing. The transformation you need to undertake involves a makeover that will erase those elements.

THE SIGNIFICANCE OF FIRST IMPRESSIONS

The entrance
Few of us stand outside our front door long enough to examine it. Yet this is exactly what potential buyers will do when they first approach your home. The first impression you create will be a lasting one in the eyes of your viewers. Bear in mind that they are likely to look at the entrance, either standing on the road outside or from the comfort of their car, for a period of time before coming to knock at the door. This aspect of your property must be welcoming and inviting. There are many simple and economical improvements you can make to achieve this. Here are a few suggestions:

- During spring and summer the installation of a few pots and hanging baskets adorned with colourful blooms will always add cheer to an otherwise bland entrance.

- During the winter months, baskets and pots can be replaced with tubs containing miniature conifers or clipped yew, bay or box, all of which will create an air of style and elegance.

- Replace rusty door furniture with new lacquered brass, which won't need constant polishing, and re-paint the door and window-frames to make the entrance appear crisp and pristine.

- Check that the door-bell is in good working order and that welcome lights operate properly.

- Replace any broken or cracked paving slabs and brighten up the rest with a suitable chemical cleaner available from most hardware stores.

- Make sure any entrance gate opens easily and shuts firmly. Repaint if necessary and oil the hinges to prevent them from squeaking.

- Ensure that the number of the property is clearly visible from the road.

- If possible avoid parking vehicles on the entrance driveway as this will obscure the front aspect of your property or, at best, it will create an obstacle that viewers will have to navigate around.

- Pay particular attention to the front garden which should be kept neat and tidy. Ensure hedges are pruned back and lawns are regularly clipped.

Estate agent's secret

A good estate agent will walk up and down the road to inspect other people's properties, assessing the comparative value and attraction of yours. If you do the same you can evaluate which are the most appealing and adapt any useful ideas, incorporating them into your own home.

The interior aspects

There are three tasks you can undertake which will instantly transform your property for the better and at nil cost. These are:

1. **Clearing away clutter.** A ruthless and determined effort to remove all clutter from your house will pay dividends. Aim for simplicity in each room and keep only those items of furnishing that are harmonious with each other. Kitchens and bathrooms are major areas of influence for buyers and, unfortunately, these are the zones most likely to be in some disarray. This rule may help: *If it has not been used in the last 12 months then you are unlikely to use it – so remove it!* If you cannot bring yourself to dispose of items, ask friends or relatives to store them for you or box them up and place them out of sight in the loft or garage.

2. **Creating a route.** Upon first entering a room almost all potential purchasers have a desire to reach the window. Examine your home and create an object-free route from the door to the window. This will encourage viewers to walk inside rather than stand at the doorway. Once at the window they will of course want to look through it, so remove any obscuring net-curtains or blinds and keep the glass spotlessly clean inside and out.

3. **Eliminating dust and grime.** Start at the top of your house and tackle one room at a time. Be methodical in your approach to this most important of tasks as once you have completed it you will need to maintain it on at least a weekly basis. Begin by examining the ceiling and remove any cobwebs and clean the light-shades. Work your way down the walls, wipe down washable wall-coverings with a damp cloth and clean or polish light-switches, sockets, pictures and shelves. The tiled areas of bathrooms and kitchens should be given special attention. Use diluted bleach or a proprietary cleaner to rejuvenate grout and polish ceramic tiles to make them

sparkle. Carpets may need professional deep-cleaning to improve their appearance but for now you could use spot stain-removers to eliminate blemishes, followed by thorough vacuuming.

Once this process is complete consider installing one or two room air-purifiers, but don't overdo it or it will become overpowering! Pot-pourri works just as well providing you remember to refresh the scented oil on a weekly basis. If you have a good sized garden why not plan now to grow strongly scented flowers that can be cut and brought indoors during your house-selling period?

If you have a budget to spend on making improvements then identify your home's greatest asset and spend it there. Popular 'features' include the kitchen, bathroom, a conservatory or garden. These areas can add appeal and value to what may otherwise be a run-of-the-mill property. For suggestions you might consider visiting a few show-homes on new-build developments nearby. Builders invariably employ professional interior designers to create contemporary and alluring living spaces, and by studying their work closely you can procure ideas with no cost to yourself.

KNOWING YOUR TARGET AUDIENCE

When considering any improvements or alterations be aware of the group of people who are likely to be your buyers. There is little point in creating a fully flagged town-garden if the majority of your neighbours are couples with young children in need of a play area. Equally a high-tech kitchen and chromed bathroom may not suit an elderly couple. Take the time needed to identify your target group and be prepared to create a home that suits their needs.

CREATING THE ILLUSION OF SPACE

In the realm of property – space is king! If you have cleared away unnecessary ornaments, furnishings, books, kitchen equipment and crockery, aerosols and lotions in the bathroom, and other such clutter, then you will already have created a home with twice the space it appeared to have before.

Space is attractive to would-be buyers. It entices them into believing they are getting value for money. It is something quantifiable. If you can fabricate the illusion of even more space then your property will be favourably compared against others that viewers may have seen in the neighbourhood. Other suggestions include:

- The age-old trick of using mirrors actually does work. A mirror not only reflects light but also doubles the depth of vision. A suitably placed mirror can make a narrow hallway appear wider and a tiny bedroom will swell in its reflection. Use them sparingly but be bold when buying – the bigger the mirror, the greater the illusion!

- Large, bulky American-style settees and chairs are comfortable but they tend to fill the living space, making the room appear small. Show-homes often use undersized furniture to suggest there is more space in the room than in reality. The same method is used in a small bedroom where a three-quarter-sized bed is installed instead of a double. The viewer fails to recognise the smaller bed and so believes the room is big enough to fit a standard double. Adapting these techniques can stretch the dimensions of your home to make it more appealing.

- Some rooms are so small that we crush furniture in to utilise them. The typical scenario is the bedroom that will just fit a double bed – providing the door is propped permanently open and a clothing-rail is used instead of a wardrobe. If this is left as it is then all you will be doing is proving to viewers that the room is too small. Clear everything out of it and leave it bare. Then explain to viewers how versatile the room could be . . . for storage, a study or dining room, a changing room or, indeed, as a bedroom.

- Large patterned floor coverings make rooms appear smaller because they allow the eye to focus on the expanse – or lack of it. Plain, light-coloured carpets or mottled small patterns reduce the eye's ability to focus on them and so rooms can appear more generously proportioned as a result.

- Dimly lit rooms with dark furniture can feel oppressive. Use the reflective quality of glass for ornaments and coffee-table tops as these will sparkle under bright lights to produce a crisp, clean and cheerful ambience.

REDECORATE TO REJUVENATE

A full or partial redecoration of your home will almost certainly be needed and if colours are chosen carefully they can further enhance the perception of space. Walk into a room with a red-painted wall and all you will see is a red wall – when what you want to see is actually the expanse between the walls. Use paint in bright pastel shades, or wallpapers with nondescript patterns, and the walls will give the impression of melting into the background.

There is good reason why magnolia outsells all other paints and has done so for many years. It is less clinical than white and provides a warm but bright background. It has a quality that causes the outer dimensions of a room to become inconspicuous, allowing the viewer to concentrate on the more important aspects.

As a general rule paint all ceilings using matt white emulsion, all woodwork with white undercoat and white gloss, and all walls in either magnolia or a light pastel colour. A good tip is to retain and store some of the paint you have used so that any marks caused later on can be easily over-painted without any shade difference.

TO SUMMARISE

- Concentrate on making improvements to the front entrance aspect of your home as this will create a good first impression for viewers.

- Remove all clutter and unnecessary furnishings to generate a feeling of space and tidiness. Spring-clean your home thoroughly from top to bottom, eliminating all dust and grime.

- Provide would-be buyers with an easy route into and through each room. Supply free access to the window area and remove anything that may obstruct the view, such as net-curtains or blinds.

- Use light-coloured, pastel-shaded paints on walls and nondescript patterned wallcoverings to further enhance the illusion of space.

3

Gathering Information

HAVING DOCUMENTS AND INFORMATION AVAILABLE

Having all the required information ready and at hand for viewers, surveyors, solicitors, mortgage lenders and headlessors is imperative if you are to keep your sanity during the sale process. A strong but compact multi-section folder in which you can store this data and access its contents easily and quickly when needed will be a sound investment.

Estate agent's secret
Estate agents will wax lyrical about local facilities and amenities without really knowing very much about them in reality. As an owner living in the neighbourhood you have a distinct advantage and practical experience of what is available . . . use it to extol the virtues of living where you do.

Legal documents

If you are an organised person you may already have most of these documents at hand or you will know where they are. If not then you will need to find them or, at worst, try to obtain copies where the originals have been lost.

- **The title deeds.** These are the legal documents that prove you own the property. If your home was originally purchased using a mortgage then they will be stored by the mortgage lender. If you purchased it without a mortgage then you or the solicitor you used to purchase the property should have them. Find out who is in possession, explain you are about to place your property on the market for sale and request the deeds in writing.

Solicitors must make a legally binding promise to return the deeds on demand (called 'an undertaking') This is governed by the Law Society. Individuals who are not solicitors are not bound by any legal sanction and therefore some mortgage lenders may be unwilling to release the deeds to them. In such an eventuality you will have to rely on your conveyancer acting for you.

- **The lease.** Unless your home was bought 'freehold' there is likely to be a Lease governing the length of term (usually 99 or 999 years) during which you can use the property. After this term expires the property ownership reverts to the 'freeholder'. The lease also contains written conditions which you as the owner are bound to observe. The original lease may have been kept with the deeds but you are likely to have been given a copy by your solicitor prior to purchase.

- **Any planning consents or variations.** If you have altered your home in some way, for example by building an extension or conservatory, then it is likely you will have had to obtain planning consent from the local authority and provide evidence of them adhering to building regulations. There may also have been some agreement for a variation, sale or transfer of land or boundary. Gather together any contracts or letters describing such changes.

- **The memorandum and articles.** If you pay a service charge and/or management charge to a landlord or management company then there will be a document detailing the regulations and rules of the company and its association with you as the tenant or lessee. It may seem strange to describe the owner of a property as a tenant or lessee but, in law, that is exactly what they are if the property was bought leasehold. Any buyer of your property will need access to the memorandum and articles and, if these documents are not held by you, your solicitor or mortgage lender, then contact the landlord or management company and ask for a copy. At the same time check whether there have been any subsequent new rules or regulations introduced affecting you and any new buyer.

- **Your mortgage documents.** Keep all up-to-date records in your file, including the name, address and telephone number of the lender, and your account and reference number. The company may have changed name and premises over the years. Double-check that your information is accurate.

Property documents

These will include:

- **Insurance policies.** The most important of these is any '*Restrictive covenant*' insurance. A restrictive covenant is a promise by the owner to use the property for certain purposes only. It may be that over the years a prior owner or yourself have inadvertently broken the terms of use through either desire or necessity, for example by rebuilding part of the property or by running a business from it or by making some fundamental alteration to a fence or wall.

When the matter is not easy to resolve, a solicitor will advise you (or any subsequent buyer) to purchase an insurance policy which protects you (or any subsequent buyer) against any losses should the covenant be enforced at some future date. The insurance now available covers a whole host of legal problems that may have arisen, for example where the landlord has disappeared or where there is a problem with the lease. The original policy is normally kept with the title deeds. Check with your solicitor whether such a policy was or will be needed and obtain the document or a copy of it for your folder.

Other policy documents to locate include any

buildings insurance, mortgage protection insurance, and any valid National Housebuilders Council Certificate (NHBC), the latter of which relates to the property rather than the owner and is therefore a policy that a new buyer will require.

- **Warranties and guarantees.** Locate all warranties and guarantees relating to work you may have had done to the property over the period of ownership. These may include installations such as double-glazing or repair work to a damp-proof course. In addition, you should retrieve any guarantees for fixtures, installations, equipment and appliances that will remain in the property after it has been sold. Some of these documents may not be transferable to the new owner or their effective term may have expired – check the wording of each document and highlight the appropriate dates or text.

- **Manuals and instructions.** These should include all property installations such as heating systems, together with instructions and manuals for fixtures, appliances and equipment being sold inclusive with the property.

Additional property information
Useful additions to your folder are minor items of information that viewers may enquire about. These could include:

- Copies of bills paid over the last 12 months for council tax, electricity, gas, water, contents insurance, service/management fees, ground rent.

- An estimate of rental value. Your buyer may be planning to let the property and, although they are likely to undertake their own research, any evidence you can supply will be helpful. Ask local letting agents to give a rough assessment and obtain details of any similar sized properties being advertised to let in the neighbourhood.

- Any useful information about the history of the property and the site upon which it stands. Has the area been used as a film or TV location? These are good talking points to introduce when viewers call. They will stimulate interest and add to the general appeal of your home.

- Use a compass to ascertain the direction that both the front and rear aspects of your property are facing. Mark this on a diagram and keep it in your folder should the question be asked.

LOCAL MERITS AND FACILITIES

Gather as much information as you can about local schools, bus and train routes, fitness and leisure centres, the nearest small shop and supermarket, health centre, dentist, the best local pub and restaurant, the nearest park and safe children's play area, and any open land for dog-walking.

It is also helpful to mark these facilities (and any others you can think of) on a large scale map showing the proximity of each to your home. Viewers will be amazed at your knowledge and impressed by your organisational aptitude . . . and they will be very grateful of the information.

USING THE INTERNET FOR RESEARCH

The Internet is an invaluable source of information for the vendor selling without an agent. The greatest problem will be to identify the items of data that are the most valuable for your document folder without being swamped under a deluge of extraneous material. The following merit a visit:

- *www.homecheck.co.uk* This invaluable site offers free environmental reports pertinent to specified post-coded areas. Aspects covered include the risk of flooding, subsidence, radon, coal-mining, landslip, landfill sites, air quality and pollution. Any adverse data should be discussed with your solicitor before disclosing to any third party.

- *www.homesight.co.uk* There is a wide amount of information available about individual neighbourhoods on this website including local house prices, school performance tables, shops and other local amenities.

- *www.upmystreet.co.uk* Another fantastic source of local information, including the effectiveness of the local authority; how crime affects the area compared with national averages; where the nearest cinema is located. This site will even tell you how to get a pizza delivered.

THE SELLER'S PACK

The government released a Consultation Paper in 1998 through the Department of the Environment, Transport and the Regions, titled *The Key to Easier Home Buying and Selling*. The outcome was a package of proposals now planned for implementation late in 2004 or early 2005 (according to the latest information from the Department of Trade, Local Government and the Regions) which is likely to change the face of buying and selling in England and Wales.

The intention of these changes is to:

- ensure that buyers and sellers are better prepared with as much information as possible right from the start

- help simplify and speed up the transaction process

- help both the buyer and seller feel more secure at an earlier stage that the transaction will go through.

Whether these proposals succeed in achieving their objective is open to debate and only time will tell. If the proposals are implemented without amendment the onus will fall on the seller to have available a variety of documents for would-be buyers to inspect. These must be prepared *before* the property is advertised or placed on the market for sale. It is estimated that the cost of producing these documents will be approximately £500 and perhaps more if particular items have to be updated over a prolonged selling period.

It may be that some firms of solicitors and estate agents will subsidise the cost of the Seller's Pack by using in-house surveyors or by obtaining information and documents electronically. The best advice would be to contact several agents and solicitors to obtain full details of their fees inclusive of compiling the pack. You can then discuss the matter with your choice of solicitor and ask what areas of the Seller's Pack you can deal with direct so that costs can be reduced.

At the time of writing it is anticipated that the seller's information pack will have to include the following:

- Copy title deeds (office copy entries) or copies of unregistered documents of title.

- A property information form containing the seller's replies to standard pre-contract enquiries.

- Replies to standard searches and other enquiries made of the local authority.

- Copies of consents relating to planning and listed building consents and building regulations.

- For new properties, copies of warranties and guarantees.

- Any available guarantees for works carried out (eg damp-proofing, timber preservation, cavity wall insulation, etc).

- A survey report on the condition of the property, including requirements for urgent or significant repairs or matters requiring further investigation.

- A draft contract.

For leasehold properties, the pack will also require copies of:

- The lease.

- The most recent service charge accounts and receipts.

- The insurance policy covering the building and receipts for premiums.

- Current regulations made by the landlord or management company.

- Memorandum and articles of the landlord or management company.

You will be pleased to note that much of this information has already been dealt with earlier in this chapter and all that should be required are one or two outstanding items that can be obtained with the help of your solicitor, plus the survey report. If you wish to save some legal expenses and speed up the selling process, read Chapter 5 which goes into greater detail about the documents required.

It is proposed that copies of all these documents should be made available for inspection by any prospective buyer – they must therefore be stored in your folder for viewing on-site or kept by your solicitor or agent who will then offer them for inspection. Once an offer has been accepted, the proposals suggest that copies of all material in the pack should be passed on to the buyer and/or his solicitor.

TO SUMMARISE

- Invest in a mobile file system in which all pertinent records and information can be stored.

- Confirm the location of legal documents and attempt to obtain copies.

- Assemble all relevant insurance policy documents, guarantees, warranties, instructions and manuals.

- Research the neighbourhood, recording the variety and location of amenities.

- Take advantage of the Internet as a source of valuable information.

- If appropriate, prepare or procure all documents required for the Seller's Pack *before* advertising the property for sale.

4

Valuing Your Property

It is said there are only two kinds of property-value statistic – the kind you look up and the kind you make up! To devise a realistic selling price for your home you will need to examine the former and guard against the latter.

USING COMPARABLES

The 'right' selling price is of course the one that buyers are prepared to pay and your task is to calculate a figure that will attract the most viewings, but not one that will lead to you underselling your investment.

Relevant local values

The market cost of property similar in size and age to your own, in the same road or closeby, will have a major influence on the value of your home. These are the 'comparables' used by estate agents to quantify property prices. To accurately assess local trends you should:

- Invite at least three local estate agents to inspect your property and obtain from them a value opinion (ensure that the agents concerned advertise this service free and without obligation).

- Visit local agents (or get a friend to do it for you if you have recently done the above) and gather together as many detail-sheets as possible of comparable property in the vicinity. Keep all the brochures you obtain as you will need them again later (see Chapter 6).

- Examine local newspapers over a period of at least a month for the advertised sale details of property similar to your own in the neighbourhood. You could also examine past copies, which are usually available at a local library.

- Walk around the area and identify any properties comparable to your own that have for sale boards erected and obtain details from the agent advertised.

- If you have Internet access visit the Nationwide national house price calculator at *www.nationwide.co.uk/hpi/calculator.asp* – which will assess the approximate current value of your home by adding the average regional increase year on year from the date of purchase. This has been tested by the author using several properties as examples and has been found to be extraordinarily accurate.

Upon completing this research you will have a number of property values from which you should choose six that closely match your own in terms of size, location, the number of bedrooms, age and condition. From these you can now record three figures:

1. the uppermost value
2. the lowest value
3. the mean average.

Contrast these with the figures supplied by agents providing you with valuations. How do they compare? The agent's figures may be more reflective of the current market situation, particularly if it is a buoyant up-and-coming region of town where prices are rising rapidly. On the other hand estate agents *always* over-value in the hope of attracting new clients and also to encourage growth in local house prices, as a result of which their percentage-based fee will also gradually rise. But remember that it may be unusual to achieve the actual asking price at the point of sale.

If the margin between the highest and lowest figures above is only slight then you can safely aim just above the mean average as a competitive target value for your home. However, if the disparity is significant then a closer examination of other influencing factors is warranted.

ADDING TO THE VALUE

There may be elements amongst the higher-priced group that are influencing the price. Examine the details to assess whether they:

- are positioned amongst other well-maintained and attractive homes

- are in an area which is locally known to be in high demand

- have a garage

- have a larger or landscaped garden area

- have a master bedroom with en-suite bathroom or shower

- have a conservatory that blends rather than contrasts with the architectural style of the building

- are south-facing or are an end-terrace or enjoy improved views due to the location on the road

- have full upvc double-glazed windows designed to be in keeping with the style and age of the property

- have a newly fitted, modern kitchen with quality fittings and appliances, or a fully-tiled bathroom with up-to-date suite and separate shower cubicle

- have an alarm system and exterior security lighting

- are well maintained and have been newly decorated throughout.

Compare your home with the above list. The greater the number that apply then the higher up your property should be placed in the valuation margin. Consider too that some elements can detract from the value. These are likely to include:

- a property in a poor state of maintenance and repair

- a badly designed extension that causes the property to appear incongruous with others in the neighbourhood

- a conservatory or extension that has taken up most of the available garden space

- a property with one or more rooms that are internal, ie with no exterior wall or window for natural light – many recently built city apartments suffer from this and it is worthwhile exploring how practical it would be to remedy the situation

- an old fashioned and outdated kitchen or bathroom

- the lack of a secure garage or the space to build one

- a property close to a railway, a motorway or busy road, fast-food outlet, factory, school playground, or similarly detrimental location.

Taking all of these into consideration you should now be able to finalise a realistic and exact valuation. Write this down together with notes to remind you how you arrived at the decision. Bear in mind that the results of this exercise may only be relevant for a short period of time, particularly in a buoyant property market. You should reappraise local prices at least once every three months to test the validity of your determination.

OTHER INFLUENCES

The national economy

When interest rates are low and the national economy forecast is bright and confident, property prices generally rise faster than the rate of inflation. If, however, the country is facing a period of economic uncertainty or a widening recession or it is anticipating a gloomy Budget from the Chancellor, property prices generally become stagnant or, even worse, they devalue. Keep up to date with the national news to assess how the country's economy is performing and take heed of what respected professionals in the field predict.

A unique or unusual property

If your home is a listed building or one of historic interest, or if it has been individually designed or is otherwise unusual, it may be very difficult to find comparable properties in the area against which a valuation can be gauged.

To obtain estimates of value you may have to widen your search to other towns or even to other counties and, if all else fails, you should rely more on the free advice given by national high street estate agents who may have experience or knowledge of similar properties they have sold elsewhere in the country.

An old property in disrepair

Depending on the extent of the disrepair it may be worth having a survey undertaken to assess what work will be needed to make it acceptable to would-be buyers. This will help in two ways:

1. It will confirm the current condition of the property and you can use the survey report to obtain estimates for any remedial work required. Once you know the costs involved you can either undertake the work yourself, which will bring the valuation back up to the local comparable level, or you can deduct the cost of the work from the identified local level for the purpose of assessing a more realistic sale price.

2. You can show the survey report to potential buyers to prove the limit of the disrepair. They will then be more confident about making an offer, being aware of the repairs and funds needed.

FINALISING THE SALE PRICE

Estate agent's secret
Never use rounded figures in an advertised sale price. If the valuation of your property is £100,000 – advertise it at £99,995. This minor adjustment can pay dividends by attracting a much greater volume of viewers.

Whatever valuation figure you have arrived at can be considered the *saleprice* . . . but this is unlikely to be the *selling price*. Bear in mind that it is common practice for offers to be made at less than the advertised price and negotiations will likely result in a selling price of about 5% below. Use this calculation when considering the finances required to fund any new purchase you may be making and, only if absolutely necessary, hike your valuation up slightly to compensate.

Always remember that raising your valuation artificially can result in a poor volume of viewings and a sluggish sale. You may have to wait for the right buyer to present themselves and then be prepared to negotiate aggressively.

TO SUMMARISE

- Obtain free valuations from local estate agents but bear in mind that these figures may be inflated above the acceptable local level.

- Find out what comparable property is selling at in your area and seek to value yours so that it is competitive within the margins.

- Fine-tune your assessment according to the condition and amenities on offer.

5

Working with Your Solicitor

Appointing your conveyancing solicitor at the earliest opportunity can pay dividends as time will be provided to create a relationship and receive advice. More importantly you can discuss how their fees might be reduced by you assisting in the acquisition and completion of various documents.

Some solicitors may not be amenable to this request, but persist and you will eventually find one who is prepared to be helpful rather than obstructive. Search for firms who have dedicated specialists in conveyancing and assess them on the quality of service offered rather than on price alone. Also ask about a *'no move no fee'* or a *'fixed fee conveyancing'* charge structure as this will prevent you paying if the sale falls through, or at worst you will avoid any additional charges being levied if it develops into a more complicated sale than first thought.

COMPLETING THE DOCUMENTS

Whilst currently there is no compulsion to provide the information suggested by the proposed Seller's Pack, this is likely to change when legislation is implemented late in 2004 or early 2005. You may wish to read the full set of government proposals available on the Internet at *www.housing.detr.gov.uk/hbs/consult* or alternatively write to the Department of the Environment, Transport and the Regions at Eland House, Bressenden Place, London, SW1E 5DU, asking for a copy of *The Key to Easier Home Buying and Selling*.

Estate agent's secret
Choose a solicitor close to where you live so that you can speak face-to-face when required. You will also save time and money (and be reassured) by handing over any completed documents personally rather than relying on the postal system.

Why complete the documents now?

Once legislation is introduced in England and Wales the documents required for the Seller's Pack will have to be made available before you advertise your property for sale. The idea is that this will speed up the legal process and offer potential buyers much more information at an earlier stage. As most of these documents will be needed regardless of legislation being introduced, it is useful to prepare them now in the event of an early sale. This will also enable you to concentrate on finding a buyer.

COPIES OF TITLE DOCUMENTS

Known as the copy title deeds (office copy entries) or copies of unregistered documents of title. Most land in England and Wales is registered by the Land Registry which is organised into 24 district registries, all of which are open to the public, though the inspection of documents is subject to a fee. You need to ascertain whether your property is registered. To do so:

- Contact the individual, company or institution that holds your deeds. This is likely to be either your solicitor or mortgage lender. Ask them whether a Land Certificate or Charge Certificate document exists. If it does then you can be assured your property is registered.

- If neither certificate can be found you will need to perform an index map search at the Land Registry by completing Form 96 which is available from a law

stationer – check *Yellow Pages* for your nearest one.
The form is also available for printing direct on the
Internet at *www.landreg.gov.uk/lrforms.asp*. When you
receive the form back from the appropriate District
Office look for an X in the box confirming that the land
is registered freehold. There will also be a title number
which you should keep safely stored for future
reference.

- Obtain Land Registry Form 109 and complete it in
  order to obtain the Office Copy Entries and Title Plan.
  You should receive a reply within a few days and the
  fee at the time of writing is a mere £4. The originals will
  be required by your solicitor once you have found a
  buyer so that a contract of sale can be drawn up. Copies
  should be placed in your document folder and Seller's
  Pack contents.

Properties are being added to the register constantly and it
may be that your property has not yet been registered.
This is more likely if your home is over 20 years old and is
in a rural area. In the event that you cannot obtain the
appropriate documents or find that it is not registered or
you know it to be leasehold, consult your solicitor who will
be able to offer advice and assistance.

THE PROPERTY INFORMATION FORM

This standard form asks you to answer a variety of
questions and is usually presented by the buyer's solicitor.
Completing it at this stage will save time later on and at
worst all you will need to do is transfer your answers onto
a different form. Questions relate to:

- Any ongoing disputes that may exist with your
  neighbours or any neighbouring property.

- The maintenance and responsibility of any boundary
  wall or fence.

- Confirmation that there is gas, electricity, water, drainage, telephone and/or cable television connected to the property and whether any run under or over a neighbouring property.

- Your liability (if any) to contribute towards any shared facilities such as pipes and drains or access routes jointly used with other people.

- Any building work you have had done or have undertaken yourself during your period of ownership and whether planning consent or building regulation approval was obtained.

- Any change in use of the building including any conversion into more than a single dwelling.

- Any guarantees associated with the property, including the NHBC certificate if appropriate.

- Current occupiers of the property, including children over the age of 16, lodgers, tenants, colleagues and guests.

Any tenant occupying your property will have statutory legal rights that may prevent you from terminating the tenancy and evicting them. Before embarking on the sale of your home you should verify that you will be able to provide the buyer with vacant possession upon completion.

If you currently do have a tenant, or any paying guest or lodger, consult your solicitor for advice before proceeding. Under no circumstances seek to harass your tenant or illegally evict them as there can be very severe penalties, including fines of several thousands of pounds.

LOCAL AUTHORITY SEARCHES

Your solicitor will ordinarily perform this essential task for you as part of the conveyancing service. It can take up to four weeks for local search results to be obtained. This is largely due to the fact that the process is performed by post and is reliant upon the efficiency of local authority staff.

The alternative is for you to do the footwork under the guidance of your solicitor, thereby executing the entire task within a single day – you can also make a considerable saving in search fees charged. The introduction of the Seller's Pack may, however, prohibit individuals performing this task and much will depend on the restrictions enforced by particular mortgage lenders.

The extent and nature of searches varies according to locality. Some will be standard whereever your property is situated, others will be dependent on various considerations including any current or prior mining of coal or tin and other such excavations, the proximity of canals and other waterways, and the position of landfill or waste-disposal sites. Consult your solicitor or a local surveyor to identify which searches are necessary.

Local Land Search

A Local Land Search is essential. Obtain Form LLC1 from your local law stationer and submit it to your local authority. Be certain to delete *'Part(s) . . . of'* in the *'Requisition for Search'* box as you want to search the entire register and not just parts of it. A reply will be expedited by you sending with the form a copy of the filed plan from the Land Registry that you should have received with the Office Copy Entries.

THE DRAFT CONTRACT

The contract makes a clear statement and an agreement about who is selling what and to whom. The draft contract sets out the same essential criteria but it is made available in advance for both parties to examine. Suggested alterations through discussion and agreement with each other are then sought and are embodied into the final sale contract.

The draft contract is not legally binding and it is

therefore safe to supply it to a would-be buyer. Although this document is not complicated to complete it is best undertaken by, or at least under the supervision of, your appointed solicitor. There are certain items of information you have already obtained which will be useful to your conveyancing solicitor so take your document folder with you when arranging this part of the procedure.

SELLING OUTSIDE ENGLAND AND WALES

This guide only relates to property being sold in England and Wales. The law affecting the sale of property in other countries, including Scotland and Northern Ireland, differs considerably and in such circumstances you must obtain legal advice from a solicitor familiar with the appropriate law of that country before proceeding.

Selling in Scotland, for example, tends to be much faster, simply because contracts become legally binding at an earlier stage and specifically when an offer is received and accepted. The documents required for a sale are similar to those in England and Wales but some have different titles and the text varies. The preparation of the property for selling is, however, substantially the same and therefore much of the advice given in this book remains relevant, with the exception of any reference to the legal process and documents required for the purpose.

TO SUMMARISE

- Employ a solicitor who is amenable to you taking an active role in the legal process.

- Negotiate a reduction in legal fees according to the amount of work you are prepared to fulfil under the supervision of your solicitor, but be careful not to cause any duplication of paperwork or complicate the process as this may lead to additional costs.

- Confirm that your property is registered with the Land Registry.

- Complete the standard Property Information Form.

- Undertake the appropriate Local Authority and Local Land searches, but check beforehand to confirm that your results will be acceptable to mortgage lenders.

- Arrange for the draft contract to be drawn up.

6

Creating a Property Brochure

The property brochure is your selling platform and primary advertisement. It is, in effect, a shop window inviting interested customers to learn more about what you are selling. It must be carefully constructed and expertly printed to attract the attention of house-hunters who are likely to have obtained scores of similar brochures.

Estate agents sometimes cut costs by photocopying property details and this is a big mistake. Photographs do not copy well and an important inducement for viewings is often lost at this early stage as a direct result. Photocopies can also blur or even obliterate text and ink-shadows can appear which further frustrate the reader. Such brochures are destined only for the waste-paper basket – whilst others of a high quality will be inspected and retained. To be certain of generating multiple viewing appointments you should set aside the maximum your budget will allow to produce a property detail brochure of the highest calibre.

Estate agent's secret
The property brochures which estate agents send to their clients for approval may appear glossy, colourful and attractive – but the version that enquirers receive could be an uninspiring and poor quality black and white photocopy. Do not lose valuable viewings by being tempted to follow this practice.

CHOOSING A DESIGN LAYOUT

The best artists in the world produce original work –
everyone else is influenced by their material and modifies
it to achieve a desired result. You can learn from
established estate agents simply by examining all the
brochures currently in your possession, decide which are
the most successful in attracting your attention, and then
profit from them by emulating the designs used.

Whilst you must be careful not to copy any design or
logo, you can identify which are the most eye-catching
colours and layouts. Narrow them down until you have
identified the best two or three and use these as a
template. Seek the opinion of several friends, colleagues
and family members to obtain a consensus of opinion. By
this stage you should have decided:

- The number of A4 pages for your brochure and
  whether it will be printed on both sides or just one
  (remember that the more pages you have the more it
  will cost to produce).

- The colour and design of any border or graphic (using
  one or two colours will be more striking than using five
  or six).

- The size and position of text including the price and
  property address.

- The size and position of the main photograph (see
  Chapter 7).

- The position and content of any bulleted text to capture
  the reader's initial attention.

DESCRIBING YOUR HOME

Be methodical in your approach

You must now identify everything in each room of your

home that you will be describing in your property brochure. This will include:

1. The structure – ceilings, walls, floors, doors, loft or attic, cellar or basement, stairways, original period features.
2. Measurements – width and length should be taken accurately in both imperial and metric (rooms with more than four walls, or walls that are not parallel, should have measurements taken at the widest points only).
3. The windows – type, double-glazing, whether south-facing, window-locks installed, curtains or blinds included, overlooking a garden or open land.
4. The decoration – newly painted, wallpapered, ceramic-tiled, textured plaster, open-bricked.
5. Fixtures and fittings – fully describe the items that will remain in the property after it is sold. These may include shelves and storage units, wardrobes, bathroom suites, shower-units, kitchen storage cupboards, light fittings, switches and sockets, curtains and blinds, mirrors, towel-rails, named appliances including ovens and washing-machines, fire-surrounds and fires, radiators, lagged water-tank and water-heater or boiler-type, telephone sockets and TV aerials, carpets and other floor coverings.
6. Exterior aspects – any garage, shed, greenhouse or covered patio. Also describe your garden areas – the sizes, whether they are stocked with mature plants and bushes, lawned areas, secure gates, fences, walls.

Chattels, fixtures and fittings

The terms used in property sales are drawn from the legal arena and much confusion is caused when reference is made to chattels, fixtures and fittings. To alleviate any doubt these are what the terms mean:

Chattels

Chattels are movable items that you can take with you when you vacate the property. There is often some duplication between what may be recognised as a chattel and what may constitute a fixture or fitting. For this reason solicitors will ask the vendor to list separately what will be staying in the property after it is sold and what they intend taking with them.

Fixtures and fittings
A fixture or fitting is something attached to the fabric of the property and which ordinarily will remain in the property when it is sold. Items might include kitchen cupboards, built-in wardrobes and curtain-tracks. Any fixture being removed prior to sale should be specified and the damage to walls repaired.

WRITING THE TEXT

Armed with your notes you can now begin putting flesh on the bones of your property brochure. When writing the main body of text you must always consider that:

- Descriptions must be brief and exact.

- Nothing should be left open to interpretation by the reader. Avoid using words like 'luxurious', 'spacious' or 'stunning', as these mean different things to different people.

- Measurements must be accurate and, where the widest points of a room are used, the words 'taken at widest points' must be inserted.

- Equipment, fixtures and fittings, furnishings, installations and appliances described in the brochure must remain in the property after it is sold.

- There must be nothing contained within a description intended to mislead the reader, for example, by stating that a switch, socket or light-fitting is made of brass when in fact it is only brass-plated or brass-coloured.

- Rose-tinted spectacles should be removed – your description must be an honest account of your home given in good faith.

- If you are in some doubt about what you will need to take with you for your new home, like carpets and curtains, leave these off the brochure and if need be you can always offer them later or even use them as bargaining elements when negotiating with a potential buyer.

Use the various brochures in your possession as a guide to format your text. Read through your drafted brochure several times and edit it down as much as possible until it contains only the essential information needed to portray your property concisely. Give prominence to the best selling features of your home and remove any reference to those elements which may discourage a sale.

Additional elements

It is always useful to add certain data about your property if space permits. Such information must be verifiable by records you have already obtained and which are being stored in your document folder. Facts given might include:

- the year the property was built

- whether it is freehold or leasehold

- the ground rent payable, if any

- the local authority to whom council tax is payable and the charge band into which your property falls

- the amount of service charge currently payable, if any, and the period covered

- the viewing arrangements and your contact telephone number.

INSERTING ESSENTIAL DISCLAIMERS

You should always add several disclaiming statements which clarify the situation and which will prevent potential conflicts or misunderstandings that could otherwise arise later on. These must include:

Statement 1

Photographs in this brochure indicate a general view of the property. It is not inferred nor must it be assumed that any items visible in the photographs are inclusive in the property sale. Interested parties must verify what is included, if anything, prior to purchase.

Statement 2

All measurements of room sizes given in this brochure are approximate and intending purchasers must not rely on them as statements of fact. Purchasers must take their own measurements prior to purchase if required for the fitting of furnishings and other fixtures.

Statement 3

The condition of all systems, installations, appliances, fixtures, fittings, furnishings and equipment have not been tested. Their condition and operation should be verified by the purchaser prior to purchase.

Statement 4

Whilst every endeavour has been made to ensure these details are accurate, the particulars are set out as a general outline only for the guidance of intending purchasers and do not constitute an offer of contract.

PRINTING THE BROCHURE

Combining the elements

How you bring all the elements of your property brochure together will depend on the facilities, finance, time and skills at your disposal. If you have access to a computer and are adept at using desktop publishing software then you may be able to complete the entire task yourself. If not, you will need to acquire some help from a friend who is prepared to undertake the exercise, or obtain professional assistance from one of the many high street design agencies.

When having the final draft printed bear in mind the following:

- You will probably need about 500 copies, which is too low a volume to make standard commercial printing economically viable. Shop around to get the best quotes or, if necessary, offer to pay for toner cartridges and get a friend to print them in shorter batches on a laser printer.

- If you have Internet access try visiting *www.printbuyers.co.uk* who offer a free service of obtaining quotes from printers throughout the UK. At the time of writing the best quote out of 20 received for providing 500 copies of a double-sided A4 full-colour brochure (excluding any design service) was £175. This price was reduced by about 20% where full-colour was used on one side only, with the remaining side printed in black and white.

- Bubblejet ink is not usually waterproof. Be certain to use a laser printer or obtain specially coated paper to fix the ink. Alternatively consider high-quality colour photocopying. Whilst you want to leave a good impression on your viewers it should not be one that stains their hands.

- Unless you use expensive photographic quality paper, you will need to leave an area of the brochure blank so that the photograph can be inserted after printing. Double check that the section left blank is the appropriate size before approving the copy for printing.

TO SUMMARISE

- Examine the property detail sheets produced by a variety of estate agents and adapt the most eye-catching design and layout as a template for your own brochure.

- Be meticulous when recording the measurements of room sizes and supply them in both imperial and metric.

- Use concise sentences when describing your property, giving priority to the best selling features.

- Recognise the difference between chattels and fixtures.

- Make it your mission to produce the highest quality brochure possible, restrained only by the budget available.

7

Photographing the Property

The photographer David Bailey, said:

'It takes a lot of imagination to be a good photographer. You need less imagination to be a painter because you can invent things. But in photography everything is so ordinary; it takes a lot of looking before you learn to see the extraordinary.'

The image that will appear on the front page of your property brochure must captivate the viewer within the first few seconds of being seen. If it is done carefully and with attention to detail, even the most mundane of residential buildings can be made to appear resplendent.

Estate agent's secret
Estate agents will always inspect all sides of a property to be sold to assess which would appear more attractive in a photograph. In some cases they will ignore a bland exterior and instead photograph an exciting interior – using this as the main brochure image.

IMAGE-CAPTURING EQUIPMENT AND FILM

Use only a high-quality camera with a good zoom lens to take your photograph. If you only possess an instamatic camera, ask a friend if you can borrow theirs or hire one from the high street. Remember that this is a once-only opportunity to acquire an image that is going to work for you – it is *not* just a holiday snapshot!

- A 35mm variable-zoom camera using a 100–200 speed roll of film will produce good results in most light conditions.

- Digital cameras are only as good as the resolution they provide. A minimum of 360dpi (dots per inch) will be needed to take a reasonable quality photograph.

- The use of a tripod will prevent any blurred results from camera-shake. If you do not have a tripod rest the camera on a wall or other nearby object when taking your picture.

- Use the zoom facility to take narrow-framed close-up shots as well as wider long-shots – but always keep your property centred in the frame.

- Be prepared to use up an entire film taking pictures from every angle of your home. Professional photographers may take 100 shots just to obtain one that is usable – there is sometimes just as much good fortune as there is skill in acquiring the ideal image.

PREPARING THE SCENE

The easiest way to ensure that your home is presented in the best possible way is to stand facing it from some distance, then inspect it carefully from the roof all the way down to the front door. The last thing you want to do is capture on film any defects such as a missing roof-tile, so ensure that these repairs are undertaken before photographing your property. You should also:

- Remove from the scene anything that may obscure the building or impair the photograph. These may include a vehicle parked on the drive; a dustbin; summer containers now with dead plants or weeds growing from them; children's toys; bicycles; the family caravan; a rotary clothes-line.

- Tidy up the garden if it is going to be in the scene – cut lawns and trim the edges; remove any weeds from borders; prune bushes and clip hedges.

- Clean all windows inside and out and draw back all curtains.

WAITING FOR THE RIGHT DAY

Be patient! Wait for a bright and sunny day before taking your photographs as this will produce the best results. Ideally have the sun striking the front aspect of your home. If it is not south-facing wait until there is a bright day when the sun is partially obscured by light high cloud, otherwise the aspect of your property being captured will be in dark shadow.

PHOTOGRAPHING DIFFICULT PROPERTIES

Even the bleakest of homes can be transformed into something wonderful with a little artistry. One of the best methods is to photograph the building at dusk, just as the sun is setting and the sky turns orange through to purple – but before it turns black. Ideally there should be a little cloud in the sky.

For this kind of scene you will need to obtain some tungsten-halogen lights to fill the foreground. These are not expensive and are readily available. Security-lights are excellent providing they have a 500w tube. Try to set up a floodlight at each end of the house and then highlight the centre doorway with a spotlight. Now turn all the internal lights and table-lamps on (except any florescents) and draw back the curtains.

Take one photo every 10 minutes or more frequently if things seem to be happening quickly. The sky is an important element in your picture so be certain you have some of it in the frame. The 'magical' moment will disclose itself on one of the resulting images after developing and you will be amazed at the dramatic effect created – and so will your enquirers.

Different types of dwelling

Detached properties are the easiest to photograph because there is a wide choice of angles and usually no neighbouring property to interfere with the setting. Others may be more problematic but it is still possible to get good results . . .

A semi-detached or terraced house

Much will depend on how attractive the neighbouring properties are. If they are well maintained then a wider shot can be taken which will partially include them in the photo, but remember to keep your own property centred in the frame. With either a semi-detached or end-terraced house take your photograph from the corner position as this will give an impression of depth and dimension.

An apartment block

Tall blocks are often best photographed from some distance. Use the zoom facility on your camera to take various shots and be aware of the surrounding scene. If possible include some green areas of open space such as a communal garden.

Getting a good position

It is often better if you can take the photograph from a position of height, but few of us have access to a helicopter so:

- look for public-access buildings nearby that you can use as a location – multi-storey car-parks are often useful for this purpose; or

- ask a local business or council office if you can gain access to the upper floors of their building; or

- book to view other apartments for sale in a nearby high-rise block and, whilst viewing, take a photograph of your own block – this may be rather deceitful but the end sometimes justifies the means.

DEVELOPING, PRINTING AND USING PHOTOS

Once you have had your roll of film developed you can choose which individual photograph depicts your property in the best possible light. Narrow them down to the best five – then employ your friends and colleagues to choose the one they prefer.

You should now have this photograph reproduced. Many high-street film-developers offer a good service at competitive prices, but shop around to get the best deal. You will need about 100 copies initially and this should cost no more than about £10. Make sure the resulting copies are at least 5" x 7" or an appropriate size to fit your property brochure. Don't be tempted to obtain mini-prints as these will fail to impress and will not do your property justice.

If you have too many photographs printed at once you may find that they become out-of-date before they can be used. A photograph taken in winter whilst there snow is on the ground should not be used on brochures despatched to potential buyers during April and May. Why? Because you will simply be confirming to them that your home has been on the market for some time and, as a result, they may believe you are now so desperate to sell that you will accept a low offer.

Photographs should be kept up-to-date, reflecting the current season so that viewers believe your home has only recently entered the market.

Attaching photos to your brochure

There are many methods and these include the use of:

- double-sided tape available from most good stationers
- permanent Photo-Mount spray available from art shops and graphic suppliers

- solid glue-sticks (not liquid glues as these will crumple the paper underneath).

TO SUMMARISE

- Using a good quality camera and the right kind of film will help you to produce the best results.

- Prepare the scene carefully – don't just snap away otherwise you and your potential buyers will be disappointed.

- Wait for a bright, dry and preferably sunny day.

- Keep photographs up-to-date by taking new ones if there is a change in the season.

8

Marketing the Property

Comprehensive marketing that exploits every opportunity to circulate information about your home is the key to a successful sale. The most sought-after product in the world will fail to sell if people are not aware of its existence. Make no mistake, the buyer of your property is already out there – you simply need to tell them where you are located and what it is that you are offering.

OBTAINING AND ERECTING A 'FOR SALE' BOARD

The importance of having an advertising sign should not be underestimated. On average 25% of all sales achieved are instigated entirely through the 'for sale' board. This figure rises considerably where the property is situated along a public thoroughfare or on a highway. Estate agents call these boards 'flags' and there is good reason . . . they signal to the buying public that your property is available to them.

The DIY approach
Making your own sign is possible but not necessarily practical. Unless you are particularly gifted with artistic skills, the cost and effort involved will probably outweigh the quality of the finished product. Those determined to create their own masterpiece should consider the following:

- Use 'correx' for the boards. This is a lightweight plastic UV light stabilised material and is resistant to most weather conditions. You should be able to obtain it in sheet form from most good graphic art suppliers.

- For the text obtain self-adhesive plastic lettering and numbers – these are available in various sizes and colours from graphic art suppliers.

- Print on both sides of the board or produce two identical boards so that the information can be displayed to face in each direction.

- If the board is to be installed in the ground, rather than fixed to a wall, paint the timber post beforehand to keep it looking smart and to prevent it from rotting in wet conditions.

Using a professional sign-maker

Decide the size of your required board (usually about 2' x 3') and plan the layout of text to be printed, then shop-around to get the best quotes from high street sign-makers. You should be able to obtain a double-sided board for about £45.

Using the Internet

Signs can be obtained direct from the Internet, though most of the ones available simply refer the viewer to a website where property details are held for public inspection.

If possible add your own telephone number to the sign using self-adhesive PVC numbers so that those unable to access the Internet can contact you direct. The cheapest sign found at the time of writing is £25.50 and can be obtained from *www.privatemove.net*

Boards that are prohibited

Local authorities determine differently the type and size of property boards that can be erected in their regions. Providing the board is not illuminated, is contained within your property boundary and does not constitute a danger or an obstruction, it will generally be acceptable. Check with the local authority planning department to identify any specific restrictions – particularly if you live in a conservation area.

Properties that are Grade I or II Listed Buildings may require written consent before boards are affixed to the external structure. Leasehold properties may require consent from the leaseholder, particularly where the only available garden is communally held and for use by all residents.

Siting the board

There is little point in going to all the trouble of creating or obtaining a sign if no one can see it, either because it has been badly positioned or because a hedge is obscuring it from view. Approach your property from every possible direction and assess the most prominent site for your board.

Once installed, check it every now and then to ensure it remains sturdy and regularly prune back any bushes that grow near it. During the winter months you will need to clean it occasionally to prevent dust and grime and even falling leaves from obscuring the all-important contact details.

EXPLOITING WORD-OF-MOUTH

Word-of-mouth is a powerful medium and one that should be encouraged and exploited. Anything that helps broadcast the fact that your property is for sale needs to be nourished at this early stage in your marketing strategy. Satisfying your neighbours' curiosity will help push your property details into many more hands – any of which could eventually sign a cheque over to you in return for the keys to your home.

The value of nosey neighbours

To be certain that your neighbours pass on accurate information to their friends and colleagues, distribute copies of your property brochure to all homes in the vicinity. If cost is an issue consider producing a simple flyer giving basic details, the price, your telephone number, the viewing arrangements, and an invitation for anyone interested to obtain the full brochure.

MARKETING TO LOCAL ESTABLISHMENTS

It is a good idea to spend a day wandering around your neighbourhood supplying various establishments with copies of your property brochure. Consider all of the following:

- Local supermarkets. Many have notice boards where customers can pin information about items they have for sale.

- Libraries. Look for notice boards you can use or leave a batch of flyers for people to pick up.

- Local newsagents. Most have a display area available free or at a nominal charge.

- Large employers. Bear in mind that 75% of people throughout the United Kingdom live within 2 miles of where they work. If there is no available notice board where you can pin your property brochure, hand a few copies in to the reception desk or send to the personnel department.

- A college or university. Try to find a notice board which most students and lecturers pass, for example one that is near to a dining room. Check whether the institution has an accommodation officer – if so, leave several copies of your brochure with them.

- A hotel. It may be difficult to get your brochures accepted by a hotel but persist and you may succeed.

- A hospital. There are always medical staff, nurses, technicians, porters and administrative personnel searching for suitable property nearby – make sure you locate notice boards in any doctors' or nurses' residence as some occupiers may be looking to move in the near future.

- Local council offices. An immense volume of people work in and pass through local authority offices. There are usually some notice boards that are open for the public to use.

Whilst visiting all of these establishments ask for the contact details and submission address of any staff newsletter or Intranet service (an in-house version of the Internet), where you can post details of your property for sale. Always keep a record of where and when you distributed property details. People are fickle and many will discard the information after a day or so. Flyers pinned to notice boards will be replaced by others needing the space. If the first flurry of enquiries fail to produce an offer, check your list and redistribute the information – preferably changing the format or colour of any circular to keep it appearing fresh and interesting.

TRADITIONAL ADVERTISING

Advertising in local publications

Advertising in local newspapers can be expensive, depending on the quality and circulation of the journal. To get the maximum response for the least expense, contact the newspaper of choice and ask about any special deals they may currently have or any that are expected in the near future. If it is a daily paper ask whether any particular edition is more popular with buyers looking for property, for example Friday's issue which is generally favoured by weekend viewers.

There will always be a number of local newsletters and pamphlets you can use to advertise your property at nominal cost and sometimes for free. Check out the local library as they often keep a stock of such publications. It is also worth visiting any nearby churches and other places of worship as these frequently produce circulars and bulletins for distribution.

Estate agent's secret

You may not need any traditional advertising if there are lots of estate agents' boards erected in your locality. These companies will be spending a small fortune on advertising your neighbours' properties. They will attract potential buyers to view them and, after viewing, those same people will look around the vicinity for similar homes on the market. Many will see your 'for sale' board and contact you for an appointment or ask for a brochure.

USING THE INTERNET FOR PUBLICITY

The Internet is a valuable source of advertising space for people selling property. There are, however, thousands of property related websites and any buyer looking for a specific type of property in a particular location can find the search process rather daunting.

The more popular websites charge for advertising space and, whilst these should not be discounted, you must make sure that any money spent is going to work for you. The best method is to act as if you were a buyer. Use a few of the search-engines such as Lycos, Yahoo and Ask Jeeves, and enter the phrase 'property for sale in (your town)'. Check the top ten results and find out whether you can advertise on those sites – identifying the cost in each case.

Free Internet advertising

At the time of writing the following sites all offer free advertising space to sellers of property in the UK and with many there is the opportunity to upload a photo of your home as well:

www.abodesonline.com
www.ad-mart.co.uk
www.estateagent.co.uk
www.findit.co.uk
www.home.co.uk
www.homes-uk.co.uk
www.housenet.co.uk
www.houses2homes.co.uk
www.housesearchuk.co.uk
www.huntahome.com
www.localbounty.com
www.notestateagent.co.uk

www.photo-ads.co.uk
www.privatemove.net
www.propertyexpress.com
www.propertyproperty.co.uk
www.property-seller.co.uk
www.readytogo.co.uk
www.reale-state.co.uk
www.suggestio.co.uk
www.thehouseexchange.co.uk
www.thepropertyjungle.com
www.yourpad.org.uk

Specialised sites

If your home falls into a particular category you should consider advertising on one of the many specialised property sites on the Internet, of which these are just a sample:

www.ukwatersideproperty.co.uk   Properties near a marina, river or canal.

www.periodproperty.co.uk   Properties of historic interest.

UNUSUAL MARKETING IDEAS

These are a few examples of the more innovative concepts that have been used successfully by sellers to promote their property:

- Suggest to a local taxi company that you will provide them with 5,000 free business cards for distribution amongst their customers, providing you can put your property and contact details on the reverse.

- If your home is on a local public transport route ask the bus company about advertising rates on the interior of their vehicles (exterior advertising tends to be expensive).

- Be ready to phone in to any live local radio or television programmes that are broadcasting a public debate. If the topic is even remotely connected with property you may be able to ask a question or make a comment and skilfully announce that your property is for sale at the same time.

- During the festive period install the biggest, brightest display of external lights you can create – then call all the local newspapers and television companies and invite them to take photographs of what you believe is the best Christmas show in town (making sure your 'for sale' board is part of the display).

- If you have a big garden offer it as a venue during the summer months for a barbecue fund-raising event to local charities and organisations. Many will take you up on the offer and all attending will see your 'for sale' sign and (hopefully) be impressed by your garden.

Use personal contacts

Take every opportunity open to you to promote the sale of your property, not forgetting your own place of work, any organisations or groups you belong to and any social gatherings you attend. For maximum effect you must aim to capitalise on every conceivable marketing occasion.

Approach investors

If there are a large number of homes and apartments to rent in your neighbourhood – and providing your own property is suitable for letting – contact local landlords who are often eager to purchase new investments. Local authority housing and environmental health departments often have lists of landlords operating in the area whom you can contact. There may also be a local authority private landlords' forum that you can attend.

In addition, there are landlords' associations up and down the country and many of these produce newsletters or magazines that welcome details of investment property. Look in telephone directories and libraries for contact details of any existing in your region.

TO SUMMARISE

- Install a 'for sale' board and ensure it is prominently positioned so that all who approach the property can see it.

- Distribute brochures or circulars to neighbours, local places of employment, education institutions and other establishments, to inform them about your property for sale.

- Use every conceivable opportunity to advertise your home and be aware of just how effective word-of-mouth can be in your marketing strategy.

- Exploit the availability of free advertising on the Internet.

9

Preparing for Viewings

Within 24 hours of your completion of the marketing strategy your telephone will start ringing with enquiries about the property. The current national average indicates that residential homes on the secondary market sell within the first 12 viewings – it can be safely assumed therefore that your buyer will be amongst the first batch of telephone calls received.

You must be prepared to deal with these calls efficiently to ensure the buyer does not slip through your fingertips. The first conversation is a starting-point and your objective here is to encourage them to book a viewing appointment. Success or failure will depend largely on how quickly you can use and adapt the three main powerful principles of selling.

THE THREE PRINCIPLES OF SELLING

Principle number 1

People do not buy products – they buy solutions to a problem!
Every purchase you have ever made is likely to have been to solve a problem. Most will have been minor difficulties, for example, there was an impending birthday and you needed to acknowledge it – so you went out and bought a birthday card because it was the easiest way of resolving the matter.

Other purchases may have been more dramatic. A new car may have solved several problems – not only did it get you to and from work every day but it also raised your status amongst friends and colleagues.

Even impulse buying is a problem-solving pastime which is why supermarkets up and down the country have last-minute opportunistic-buying displays near the cashier's till. The array of goods presented are there to help prevent you from getting bored whilst waiting to be served on busy days. The chocolate treats, magazines and special offers distract you for a few minutes – just long enough for you to reach the front of the queue.

Although these minor acquisitions pale into insignificance when compared with buying a new home, the principles involved are identical. Your prospective purchaser has a problem – they are relocating for a reason – your objective is to expose the problem and resolve it with the product you have available.

Principle number 2

People cannot shake hands or sign a contract with a clenched fist!
You must try to convince enquirers that you are an honest, trustworthy and friendly seller. If telephone enquirers are presented with someone brusque or arrogant they will feel threatened and become defensive. Even worse, they are likely to end the conversation abruptly without booking an appointment to view.

You should metaphorically extend a welcoming hand in the tone of your voice. It may sound absurd but smiling as you talk will project pleasant inflections in your voice that the caller will find both attractive and appealing.

Emotively create a friendship between you and the caller and, providing the property satisfies their needs, you will be increasing the chance of successfully selling it to them. The reason for this is that whilst it is very difficult to say 'no' to a friend who you trust and respect – it is very easy to say it to a stranger for whom you have little but contempt.

> **Estate agent's secret**
> Estate agents recognise that a cheerful and professional telephone manner can help create an instant rapport with an enquirer. Your demeanour really does matter – practise smiling whenever you answer the telephone and see the difference it makes by the responses you receive.

Principle number 3

If the product doesn't fit the buyer's needs – try to make it fit!
By listening to what the purchaser is looking for you should be able to assess which qualities of your property will satisfy the most. If there are elements missing then examine the structure closely to see whether minor alterations can be made by the buyer to create a perfect home.

The typical scenario is where a potential purchaser suggests that *'it would be ideal if only there was another bedroom'*. If they can be convinced that another bedroom could be established easily and cheaply by installing a dividing wall in the biggest bedroom, then a sale could still be achieved.

PREPARING FOR TELEPHONE CALLS

When answering the telephone to enquirers have at hand:

- a notepad and several pens (in case one fails whilst writing)

- your document folder with information about the property and the neighbourhood

- a copy of the property brochure giving details of room sizes

and . . .

- turn the television off if the telephone is in the same room

- if possible ask a partner or family member to keep young children quietly occupied

- close any nearby windows to keep exterior sounds to a minimum and particularly any noise from traffic, barking dogs, car-alarms and children playing.

SECURITY AND SAFETY ISSUES

Beware the bogus caller

Unfortunately not all telephone calls you receive will be from genuine house-hunters. There are those who prey on owners selling property, operating in the knowledge that there are opportunities to commit theft by posing as interested buyers. You must take every precaution to guard against such individuals entering your home.

These unscrupulous characters are very practised in deceit and will at first appear as genuine purchasers. Estate agents use a simple procedure that successfully defeats would-be criminals in 99% of all cases.

After booking a viewing appointment, ask the caller to provide you with their:

- full name

- telephone number

- first line of address

- his post-code.

If there is any hesitation between giving the first line of their address and the post-code, you can be almost certain the caller is bogus. The reason is that all genuine callers will immediately know their post-code whilst dishonest ones will need a short amount of time to concoct a false one. It is a simple technique – and it works!

If you have Internet access you can double-check whether the first line of the address and the post-code match by going to *www.royalmail.com* – this is a free service. You should also telephone the caller the day before the appointment to check that the number supplied is genuine.

When making arrangements for a viewing do not under any circumstances state that an appointment cannot be made due to your being at work during the day, or because you are going on holiday, or that you will be out of the property at the time requested. This simply provides criminals with knowledge of an empty house. Instead state that it is not convenient due to you having guests staying with you at that time.

Your own personal safety is even more important than the security of your property and we will discuss this in more detail in the next chapter.

SEARCHING FOR ANSWERS

Whilst the first conversation with your caller should never be allowed to progress into an interrogation there are questions you can ask, if the opportunity arises, that will greatly assist you later on. These include:

Are you looking to move to this area specifically?
Have you already sold your own home?
What is it about this property that attracted you?
How did you find out about this property?
Are you familiar with the area?
Is it just for yourself or do you have a family?
Do you have a car?
Do you work nearby?
Will you need a mortgage to buy a property?
Would you like me to send you a property brochure?
When would you like to come and view my property?

The answers to these questions will provide you with an insight into the buyer's aspirations, their ability to buy a property, the elements of a property that are important to them and their level of interest in your home. Furthermore they will also suggest areas that you can later expand on to encourage an offer. It may be useful to have these questions written down, along with any others you think may be useful, so that you can refer to them during calls.

MAKING A VIEWING APPOINTMENT

You should attempt to satisfy the enquirer's ideal viewing date and time but not if it will be detrimental to the presentation of your property. It may be, for example, that at certain times and on particular days there is a considerable amount of traffic passing in front of your home. This would clearly deter a would-be buyer and therefore an alternative time or day would be favourable.

You might also elect to arrange appointments when young children are at school or with family members and when you know that the dog will be out being exercised.

USING TELEPHONE ANSWERING MACHINES

A missed call is a missed opportunity and because you cannot be available 24 hours a day, seven days a week, an answering machine is an inevitable necessity. When using such a facility remember to:

- Make sure that your announcement does not indicate you are out of the house – it should simply state that you cannot answer the telephone at the current time but will call them back if they leave a name and number.

- Refrain from using gimmicky prerecorded messages as not all callers may find them entertaining or appropriate.

- Keep the announcement short and simple.

- Call people back as soon as possible after receiving a message. If you allow several days to pass by the caller may already have looked at other properties of interest and could even have submitted an offer on one of them.

Keeping a record

In the first few weeks of putting your property on the market you are likely to receive a deluge of telephone calls, most of which will lead to viewing appointments being made. Be certain to write them on a calender so that you know who is coming, and when, and keep a concise record of the conversations you have had, including any bits of information acquired which may prove useful later on.

TO SUMMARISE

- Treat each and every telephone call as though you are talking to a potential buyer – be polite and friendly.

- Attempt to gain as much information from the caller as possible without turning the conversation into an interrogation.

- Be prepared to supply information from your document folder to encourage a viewing.

- Be aware that not all callers are genuine – some may be looking for an opportunity to commit a crime.

- Book viewing appointments that will show your property under the best possible conditions.

10

How To Conduct A Viewing

If all has gone according to plan, the first viewing has been booked, the children are at school, the dog has been fostered out to friends and a warm and welcoming glow is radiating from an open fire in the living room. The show-house has been meticulously prepared and is now ready for inspection.

MEETING AND GREETING YOUR VIEWERS

Be prepared for diversity
Every viewing you conduct is likely to be different from the one that preceded it. The range of people who come to tour your home will be diverse. Some will be unaccompanied although most will attend with a spouse, partner or friend. Occasionally an interested buyer may bring his entire family with him including parents, grandparents and grandchildren. I have actually experienced one where the viewer even brought along his pet dog! Most will be polite and friendly. One or two may appear hostile and intimidating. For some it will be the first viewing of a property they have attended whilst for others your home may simply be the latest on a very long list.

Regardless of the face or faces that you see upon first opening the door . . . smile amiably, introduce yourself by name and welcome them into your home. Always bear in mind that these could be your buyers!

Take the initiative

This may be the only occasion during the entire viewing when you have the upper-hand and you should use the opportunity to create a good first impression. Direct your guests towards the most awe-inspiring room in your home. This may be a living-room with panoramic views; a modern newly fitted and spotlessly clean kitchen; a bright conservatory overlooking the garden; or it may be the entrance hall where you are currently standing.

ANALYSING BODY LANGUAGE

You can learn a great deal about your viewers by observing them as you enter each room. Whilst some will be direct and talk openly about your property, others may be more reluctant, preferring to be polite rather than honest. Few will however be sufficiently practised to prevent an expression giving away their true feelings. Look for positive reactions to particular rooms or specific features and raise them in conversation later to reassert their value.

Your own body language is also important to the success or failure of each viewing. Once you have invited your guests into a room allow them to take the lead and move ahead of you in the direction of their choice. Most will advance towards a window to examine the exterior view before turning to inspect the interior aspects. Stand back a little, indulge in conversation and allow them time to talk to each other. Use this opportunity to point out any particularly attractive features you believe they may have overlooked.

When they are ready to move on they will signal by walking towards the door. Move in front of them if you can and lead them towards the next area.

> **Estate agent's secret**
> Estate-agents usually invite buyers to enter a room in front of them. With no other people in view the room can appear more spacious and less cluttered. Use this technique when you are showing your own home to create a better first impression.

DEALING WITH DISRUPTIVE CHILDREN

Young children become bored very quickly and some parents fail to keep them under adequate control whilst viewing properties. This can result in disruptive and potentially hazardous behaviour. If allowed to go unchecked these little bags of bedlam can cause untold damage to themselves and to your possessions. You should be polite – but you should also be firm! A strong and authoritative *'please don't do that'* is usually enough to improve their conduct. This also demonstrates to the parents that you will not tolerate unruly behaviour in your home.

SAFETY AND SECURITY

It is of vital importance that you adopt and maintain a high level of caution when inviting strangers into your property. Whilst most viewers will be genuine there are those who could abuse the situation and use it as an opportunity to commit crime.

- Remove jewellery, cash, creditcards, cheque books and bank statements, keys, and any other valuables or material containing personal data to a safe and secure place.

- Supervise the movement of viewers and keep them under strict and close observation at all times.

- If you cannot arrange to have a partner, friend or relative to be with you during an appointment be certain to inform someone that it is taking place. Explain that you will telephone them at an agreed time once the viewing has ended or get them to contact you.

- Despite questions that may be asked, do not divulge any details about times or days when you are likely to be out of the property and under no circumstances explain the operation of an alarm-system.

- Carry a personal attack alarm with you whilst showing the property.

- Never accept unannounced viewings. If interested parties knock at your door having seen the 'for sale' sign, take their details and make an appointment for another day.

- If a viewing is taking place during the early evening keep curtains in the open position and turn all internal lights on.

Protecting your home

Dry and sunny days are a seller's dream. But sadly the weather is inclined to turn wet from time to time and this will result in people arriving with muddy shoes and dripping coats. This can easily be dealt with by investing in some good quality doormats and offering to hang up any rain-drenched garments.

Umbrellas can also be a nightmare. Where do you put them? An umbrella-stand is ideal but equally a large floor-vase will suffice and prevent your carpets and wall-coverings from getting soaked.

LISTENING TO WHAT PEOPLE ARE SAYING

Viewers will often disclose information about themselves without realising it and it is therefore essential that you listen to what is said. Something that may appear quite insignificant at the time could prove to be crucial later during the negotiation stage.

Dealing with awkward questions

Potential buyers will be keen to acquire information about you and your home and are likely to ask some difficult and searching questions during the tour. Some of these enquiries can be answered openly as they will encourage an offer, whilst others will need to be avoided. Remember the golden rule . . . recognise the demand and supply it . . . only give an answer if you are certain it is what your viewer wants to hear. Some typical questions include:

How long has your property been on the market?
What they are really asking is *'How desperate are you to sell?'*. If it has been less than a month then you can afford to answer honestly. On the other hand if it has been advertised longer then you should be more vague in your response. *'Only a short time'* is a useful reply for this situation.

Is the washing-machine staying?
Buyers always like to believe they are getting the best possible bargain – if leaving an appliance will achieve a sale at or close to the asking price then clearly it is worth conceding on such matters.

Can I knock this wall down to make a bigger room?
Never be tempted to reply to such enquiries (unless you happen to be a structural surveyor). If you do not know the answer – don't guess at it!

Would you accept an offer?
Although you probably would, never appear too keen as it will severely impair your negotiating position. Simply suggest that you will *consider* any reasonable offer subject to the buyer being able to achieve exchange and completion within an acceptable time period. Bear in mind

that many purchasers seek to reduce an offer made if survey findings are detrimental – so it may be expedient for both sides to wait until such results are known before finalising any agreement on price.

Why are you moving?
Be careful with this one as you don't want to discourage a sale by telling them about noisy neighbours or the construction of a new motorway nearby. This question can be dealt with by explaining you need more or less space, that you need to relocate to advance your career, or some other circumvented reply.

BRINGING THE VIEWING TO AN END

Lasting impressions also count
Just as important as the first room your guests entered when they arrived is the last one they see before they leave. On a warm day this could be the garden which is a safe and suitable place to leave them alone for a short time so that they can discuss the virtues of your property in some privacy.

Viewers will indicate when they wish to leave but before they do:

- check you have *their* full contact details

- check that they have a property brochure with *your* contact details

- invite them to return for another viewing

- ask if there is a room they would like to look at again before they leave

- only if you are confident that all your valuables are safely out of reach consider inviting them to look around on their own

- explain that you will telephone them in a few days if

you don't hear from them beforehand so as to obtain some useful feedback.

Saying farewell

Don't be tempted to escort your guests down a driveway or to a vehicle as this may prevent them from loitering. Interested viewers will wish to look back at the property from a nearby vantage point to discuss its merits and suitability – your presence during this time will simply discourage them from staying on-site.

TO SUMMARISE

- Always welcome viewers with a smile regardless of what meets you when opening the door.

- Make the first and last rooms entered ones to remember.

- Take steps to ensure your own safety and also the security of your property.

- Encourage conversation and remember to listen to what your viewers are saying.

- Don't rush the viewing! Give potential buyers time to inspect everything and, if possible, provide them with a period of privacy.

11

Receiving Offers

An offer for the purchase of your home will be submitted
either at the end of a viewing by an aggressive buyer or,
more likely, by telephone within a few days. Although you
can justifiably feel jubilant in receiving an offer you should
be aware that this is only the start of a long and formidable
path. Completion of the sale has many stumbling blocks
yet to overcome before the offer can be considered secure.
These include:

1. Negotiating up and down to reach an agreed selling
   price.
2. Negotiating again in the event of a detrimental buyer's
   survey or valuation.
3. Agreeing a time-scale for exchange of contracts.
4. Keeping any buy/sell chain intact during the period to
   completion.
5. Overcoming any delays that might occur.
6. Responding to any last-minute enquiries and concerns
   raised during the legal process.
7. Arranging for the purchase of your new home (if
   appropriate) to coincide exactly with the dates of
   purchase proposed by your buyer.
8. Being prepared to consider any additional higher or
   more secure offers from alternative buyers that may be
   presented before completion is attained.

BUYERS TO BE CAUTIOUS OF

Be wary of the aggressive buyer
Aggressive buyers will ask you lots of questions during a

viewing because they need to assess how desperate you are to sell. The more disheartened you are – the lower the offer is likely to be. They will also point out all of the aspects of your home that are unsatisfactory or defective and attempt to impress upon you that the chance of achieving a sale at the asking price is dubious at best.

Aggressive buyers will make lots of promises. They will tell you they can complete within weeks, have cash funds in place and have no property to sell. Some will apply added pressure by stating that the offer made is time-dependent and only available if you accept it within a number of days. Some will even make the offer at the end of a viewing and ask you to accept it there and then.

Offers made by such buyers are usually between 15% and 20% less than the asking price. Make no mistake – these are the last people you should sell to unless your property has been on the market for several months with no other interested parties to be seen. Also known as 'cash buyers' these investors are professional negotiators who earn a living by undermining the actual value of property; they buy it cheaply, then they either rent it out or sell it on at a higher market price.

Never accept an offer face-to-face. If you are at all tempted by an aggressive buyer . . . take the time needed to consider the positive and negative aspects of their proposal thoroughly over a number of days. This will also provide you with an opportunity to gather information about them and, properly armed, you can then assess the validity of any promises they have made.

'Cash-buyers' rarely exist

The lure of a cash-buyer is that the purchase will be uncomplicated. They are not involved in a chain, may not require a survey, and once a sale-price is agreed it is unlikely to be revised due to an inadequate mortgage valuation.

If only life were so sweet! In reality cash-buyers are more likely to:

- Apply for a mortgage at a later date than most other buyers and at a time when you are unlikely to back out.

- Have no actual cash at all – they may however have financial assets such as stocks and shares or bonds which they will need to sell before they can proceed.

- Have some cash but will need to top this up with a combination of the above.

Even if they are genuine cash-buyers and really do have money in the bank they will not want to part with it. As a result their offer is likely to be very low and any negotiations will be undertaken aggressively. If a so-called 'cash-buyer' presents themselves to you ask for evidence of their claim including sight of bank statements or a letter from the bank confirming they have sufficient and immediately accessible funds to buy your home.

BUYERS WORTHY OF ENCOURAGEMENT

Emotional buyers are amongst the best you could ever wish to find. They will often call for a second viewing (and sometimes even a third and fourth after that) before making an offer. Many will be first-time buyers living with their parents or in rented accommodation and who now believe they have found their dream-home. Others may have been looking for something suitable for months before discovering your property and all that it has to offer. These buyers don't just like your property – they 'love' it – and that emotional attachment can work strongly in your favour because:

- Securing the purchase will be a higher priority than saving money through making a low offer.

- They will want to complete the purchase quickly to prevent anyone else acquiring the property and may even offer the asking price right from the start.

- Having *'fallen in love with it'* they will be eager to occupy the property and turn it into their home at the earliest possible opportunity.

- Even if their own funds are stretched or a mortgage application falls short of requirements, emotional buyers are often prepared to make an extraordinary effort to achieve completion at any cost.

Estate agent's secret

Estate agents are good negotiators simply because they are not personally or emotionally involved in the sale. If you are under stress you will fail to negotiate effectively. As an alternative, ask a friend or relative to become the mediator between you and the buyer during this crucial stage.

ADOPTING AN EFFECTIVE ATTITUDE

Feign complacency en route to success

Eagerness, excitement and anticipation are a seller's worst enemy. If a buyer discovers these traits they will use them against you in any negotiations that follow. Try to stay calm and if necessary contrive apathy in any conversation with them. This will have the effect of raising the odds in your favour and lead them into thinking there is another offer on the table – and that you are confident about a sale proceeding whether or not they stay in the picture.

Once an offer is received and regardless of the amount, write it down and take the buyer's contact details. Explain that you will consider it over the next few days before telephoning back with a response. Now check the notes you made earlier and assess the level of interest, the quality of offer and the strength of their buying position. Ask the question: *'Do I need more information?'* If so, seek to obtain it before proceeding any further.

Once you have all the required data, balance it against an offer that you would ordinarily be prepared to accept.

Whilst it may be difficult to quantify the value of someone who does not require a mortgage, or is not involved in a chain, or who is clearly keen to proceed, these qualities are significant and merit consideration. It is often worth accepting a slightly lower offer from a strongly positioned buyer than from one of more substance but who is in weak, vulnerable or uncertain circumstances.

CALCULATING A RESPONSE TO OFFERS

After three or four days, and assuming the buyer has not contacted you in the meantime, contact them and supply your response. The buyer will almost certainly expect you to meet them somewhere in the middle of the two figures and it is always worth suggesting the mid-point plus 50% of the difference. For example:

(A) Property for sale at:	£100,000
(B) Offer received at:	£ 90,000
Difference:	£ 10,000
Mid-point of A and B + 50% of the difference =	£ 97,500

Most buyers will return after some 'thinking time' with a new offer slightly less than the one you suggested. In the example above an agreed selling price could be anticipated at £96,500 which is just 3.5% less than the asking price – this compromising formula and the resulting outcome provides a generally high degree of satisfaction for most vendors and most buyers.

Keeping the offer alive

If the buyer's final offer is still below a figure you have decided would be acceptable, there is no easy way of proceeding and you should turn your attention back to marketing and viewings. However, do not cut all ties with the person making the offer – promise to contact them should circumstances change or if a buyer has not been found within the next couple of months. This will create an avenue of opportunity for you in the event of there being no further offers.

Of course, by that stage the buyer may well have found an alternative property or, at best, will probably reduce their original offer even further knowing that gloom and despair are creeping in. It will nonetheless provide you with an option that you can accept or reject – and it is always better to have something available waiting in the wings rather than nothing at all.

GAZUMPING AND GAZUNDERING

Avoiding a gazumping situation

Gazumping occurs when a seller agrees to accept a higher offer from an alternative buyer *after* agreeing to sell the property to someone else, subject to contract. It is a term that evokes despondency in estate agents because:

- Gazumping creates bad feeling between the vendor and the initial buyer, particularly if it happens after expenses have been incurred for a survey and mortgage application.

- It destroys trust between the parties and makes the sale volatile and precarious.

- Even the new buyer will feel they are dealing with someone who cannot be relied upon to be honest and open about completion being achieved.

- The initial buyer rarely returns if the new purchaser withdraws – leaving the vendor with no one to sell to.

Although there is nothing illegal about gazumping it is considered by most to be an unprincipled act (even unethical in some quarters) and is usually best avoided. The outcome is rarely satisfactory and there is always risk involved. Provided the original buyer is proceeding with the purchase at an acceptable pace, has already had the survey and/or valuation conducted, has a mortgage offered and is not involved in a fragile chain, then you can be reasonably confident of them advancing through to completion. Stay with this buyer in preference to starting again – aspiring to make a small financial gain is unlikely to be worth the gamble.

Gazumping is unlikely to be eradicated by the new Seller's Pack legislation due to come into force late in 2004 or early 2005, as there is nothing contained in the current proposals which will prevent a continuation of this calamitous practice.

Protecting yourself from being gazundered

Gazundering occurs more often than many people think. This is an atrocious practice whereby a purchaser reduces their offer just before the sale completes. The seller is often devastated – and rightly so – because they are likely to have everything else in place ready for moving, including the purchase of a new home. The vendor is effectively cornered with two choices, either to:

1. Accept the reduced offer, absorb any deficit in funding or take out a bigger loan for the new home, and complete the sale.

2. Reject the reduced offer and submit to the risk of losing the buyer together with all the implications involved, including the loss of the new home, and with considerable legal and other expenses having been incurred.

To avoid being gazundered you should make every attempt to expunge the capabilities the buyer has to reduce their offer during the sale process. These might include:

- Providing the buyer with a copy of your survey report as soon as they make an offer. The report will explain any defects and, once known, they will become redundant as excuses for reducing the agreed purchase price later on.

- Receiving confirmation from the buyer that they have arranged for and had a survey and/or valuation undertaken. Having paid for these they will be reluctant to withdraw without good reason.

- Having sight of written evidence that the buyer has received a suitable mortgage advance for the property.

- Creating a friendly relationship with the buyer, making it much more difficult for them to thwart you at the last minute.

- Keeping your property active on the open market and refusing to take down the for sale sign until exchange of contracts has taken place.

Survey and valuation reports

It is not uncommon for an offer to be made and agreed and then lowered due to a detrimental survey report and/or a resulting under-valuation. The buyer will often quote defects identified and suggest that their new offer is based on repair estimates received.

If this is genuine, rather than a ploy to acquire the property at a reduced price, they will not object to you having sight of the survey and valuation reports and the estimates. Once these are in your possession you can decide whether to complete the repairs at your own expense, thereby keeping the original offer at the same level, or accept the lower offer bearing in mind the cost of work needed.

On the other hand, if the buyer refuses to hand over evidence of their claims you would be rightly justified in being suspicious about them. The question is, were you aware of the defects (through living in the property or by having your own survey undertaken) and if so have you considered them when calculating the offer price of your property? If you have, there is no need to accept a reduced offer – show the buyer your calculations set against comparable property in the area and leave them to contemplate the facts.

Don't take insults personally

Buyers will often resort to making disparaging remarks about you and your property in a bid to lower the price. You should always keep in mind that this is a game they are playing and if you allow your emotions to get the better of you . . . they win! Try to keep calm and if necessary end the conversation quickly but politely to prevent an argument developing. You can always call them back once you are in a better frame of mind.

TO SUMMARISE

- Keep calm during negotiations and remember that buyers will try to justify a low offer by describing the adverse qualities of your home.

- Be wary of aggressive 'cash-buyers' – the promises they make rarely live up to expectations.

- Review the information you have gathered to assess the strength and quality of a buyer set against the offer they have made.

- Always encourage a buyer who displays an emotional attachment to your property.

- When negotiating – aim high but be prepared to compromise.

- Never appear too keen to provide a response after the initial offer has been made – an outward sign of complacency will keep you firmly in the driving seat.

- Avoid a gazumping situation and try to protect yourself from being gazundered.

12

Heads of Terms

The Heads of Terms is the draft contract the solicitor draws up at the start of the legal process when selling your property. It contains the most important elements – but not all of the fine detail. There are various items of information you need to supply to your solicitor and to the buyer's solicitor in order that this process can begin. These are:

- contact details for all involved parties; and
- basic facts about the property being sold.

RECORDING DETAILS REQUIRED BY SOLICITORS

If you do not have access to a computer or typewriter, write the following details in black ink and use block capitals to prevent any misinterpretation when they are read by your buyer and by each other's solicitor. At the top of the page write '*Heads of Terms Details (Subject to Contract)*' then record the data in the order they appear below, using the underlined heading for each element:

THE VENDOR
Write your full name including your title, for example, 'MR JOHN MICHAEL SMITH'. If there is a joint-owner or co-owners enter their full names to the right-hand side on the same line.

VENDOR'S ADDRESS
Directly underneath your name enter your correspondence address which may or may not be the same as the address

of the property being sold. Be certain to include your post-code as this will ensure the fastest possible postal delivery when letters and other documents are sent to you. Repeat the same process, placing the relevant correspondence address under the joint-owner or any co-owners' names.

VENDOR'S CONTACT DETAILS

Following the same column-line downward enter all available contact telephone numbers, facsimile number and any e-mail address under each name and address. If you record different telephone numbers under this heading be certain to explain any that are only available at certain times, for example, *'only during the day'* or *'only after 6pm'*.

POINT OF CONTACT

If there are two or more owners of the property it is helpful for one to be identified as the *'point of contact'*, that is, the person with whom the solicitor will ordinarily liaise, send information and ask questions of. This will greatly speed up the process but there must be an agreement between the owners for this to happen, particularly if they are unrelated or live in different locations. Where an agreement has been reached enter, *'It is agreed between the owners that all communications regarding the sale of our property should be addressed to (enter the appropriate name)'*.

THE PURCHASER

Record the name of the purchaser in the same manner as you did for 'THE VENDOR'. Be certain to obtain the full name and check that the spelling of it is accurate. Ask about any joint-purchaser or co-buyers and enter their names to the right-hand side if appropriate.

PURCHASER'S ADDRESS

Directly underneath the name(s) enter the home address(es) of the purchaser(s) together with the post-code. The address(es) should be the *registered* location(s) of the buyer(s) and not merely a place of employment or somewhere they collect mail from.

PURCHASER'S CONTACT DETAILS
Under each name and address write the telephone number, facsimile number and any e-mail address.

THE PROPERTY BEING SOLD (subject to contract)
Enter the full address of the property and the post-code.

AGREED SALE PRICE (subject to contract)
Record the price agreed between you and the buyer in both numbers and words, for example, '*£100,000 (one hundred thousand pounds sterling)*'.

INCLUSIVE OF . . .
Enter here the fixtures, fittings, appliances, equipment and/or furnishings that you are providing inclusive within the price of the property and which have been agreed with the buyer. If specific appliances are being left make sure to list them by naming the manufacturer, model and design number, or some other easily identifiable description. If only some carpets are being left, distinguish them by recording the appropriate room, for example '*blue patterned carpet in the living room*'. Careful and exact descriptions will help to prevent any potential conflicts or misunderstandings arising later on.

After you have listed all inclusive elements, write directly underneath: '*All items listed are being provided as seen and no warranty or guarantee of operation or condition of any fitting, fixture, installation, system, appliance, equipment or item of furnishing will be given by the vendor. It is advised that the buyer undertakes to have any items professionally tested at their own expense as appropriate before completing the purchase.*'

VENDOR'S SOLICITOR
Enter the full name and address of your solicitor along with all contact telephone, facsimile and e-mail data. If

there is a particular solicitor within the practice who has been appointed to deal with your sale, write the subheading *'Person To Contact: (enter name here)'*.

PURCHASER'S SOLICITOR
Register the appropriate name, address and contact telephone, facsimile and any e-mail address in the same manner as you did when writing your own solicitor's details.

ADDITIONAL PROPERTY INFORMATION
Under sub-headings record any of the following which are relevant:

Tenure
Whether the property is *'freehold'* or *'leasehold'* – if the latter, enter the number of years outstanding if known or alternatively write *'the remainder of (number of years)'*.

Leasehold information
If the property is leasehold, record the name, address and telephone number of the headlessor.

Management company
If a service charge or management charge is being paid, enter the name, address and telephone number of the management company or any agents who are being employed to collect such fees from you.

Service charge and/or management charge
Write the amount being paid and the period it covers, for example, *'£810 payable in 12 instalments of £67.50 on the 15th day of each month. This is for the period 15th August 2002 to 14th August 2003 inclusive.'*

Ground rent
If ground rent is being paid enter the details to whom it was last paid. Also add the date and amount of the last payment and, if known, the frequency of collection.

ESTATE AGENT

If you have opted to use this book to save yourself thousands – enter *'None'*.

TIMESCALE

Write here any pertinent assurances, comments or promises made by yourself and the buyer. For example: *'The buyer has stated that he has no property to sell and he is not therefore involved in a chain. He has added that his purchase will be dependent upon a favourable mortgage advance being made and that he has already submitted his application to (name of lender).'*

Also record here: *'Both parties are seeking the earliest possible exchange of contracts with completion proposed within 21 days thereafter.'*

POSSESSION

Enter (unless your property is being sold with a tenant in occupation): *'The vendor confirms that the property is to be provided with vacant possession upon completion.'*

Under the last line of text write *'Vendor's Signature'* and then date and sign the page. Under your own signature write *'Purchaser's Signature'*.

PREVENTING DELAYS

Delays in the sale process can occur because:

- Solicitors receive the wrong information from the vendor or the purchaser at the very start of the legal process.

- The vendor or the purchaser misinterpret the negotiated sale particulars and make an assumption about the price, the property and what is included. This information is then acted upon by solicitors and the mistake is only identified late in the sale.

- Verbal assurances given by the purchaser that they can achieve completion quickly and easily, because they have no property to sell or no mortgage required, are later found to be false or misleading.

- The buyer fails to adequately provide their solicitor with the correct information about the vendor, contact details for the vendor's solicitor and/or full data on the property being purchased.

These delays can all be prevented by sending the buyer two copies of the Heads of Terms details you have prepared. If they can receive and send faxes use this medium because it will save time. In a covering letter or by telephone ask the buyer to check the details for accuracy and then sign in agreement where indicated, before returning one copy to you.

Once you are in receipt of a verified, signed copy the purchaser is unlikely to raise questions later on and as a direct result most delays will be avoided.

Estate agent's secret
Estate agents are often amazed at sellers who instruct their solicitor and then leave for two weeks' holiday without informing anyone. If you are going to be unavailable, even for a few days, be certain to let your solicitor and the buyer know about it. This will help prevent any anxiety that may otherwise be caused where an enquiry has been issued but no response received.

WHO SHOULD RECEIVE COPIES?

Send one copy to the buyer's appointed solicitor and one to your own. If you send these by standard mail delivery always telephone to confirm they have been received – there are an extraordinary number of documents said to have been 'lost in the post' and, whilst this defence may be considered suspect, it is nonetheless a reason given for many delayed sales.

PROVIDING SUPPLEMENTARY DATA

Your solicitor will require further information from you and it is a good idea to provide this at the same time as the Heads of Terms details. Such information might include:

- An up-to-date record of your mortgage lender's name and address, your account and/or reference number, and a copy of the last statement you received from them.

- A copy of the last receipted payment of ground rent (if any) or details of how much is payable and to whom it is normally paid.

- If there are currently tenants occupying the property, a copy of the tenancy agreement together with any Notice to Quit that may have been issued.

- An up-to-date statement of any service charges paid, together with a calculation of the amounts anticipated to become due up to the expected completion date.

- All other information or details identified in prior chapters which should be available from your document folder.

WHAT HAPPENS NEXT?

After all your hard work marketing the property, finding a buyer, negotiating a sale price and instructing solicitors, you might think that you have earned a rest. Although you may well deserve it – this is not the time for contentment!

Some solicitors are excellent. They will act for you in an efficient and proactive manner, forcing the sale forward and communicating the success of each stage as soon as it has been executed. Others are not so adept at keeping you informed and may even fail to progress the sale if they have a backlog of transactions under way. Most will fall somewhere in between.

One thing is common amongst all conveyancing solicitors – they detest being continually disturbed by clients eager to find out what is happening with their sale or purchase. Whilst it can be beneficial for you to make a nuisance of yourself (because they will dearly wish to bring the sale to completion at the earliest rather than the latest opportunity so as to rid themselves of the aggravation), at the same time you must be careful not to harass them so much that they become frustrated and evasive.

Your solicitor should write to you within the first few days of being issued with the Heads of Terms details. They should explain what they are doing to set the legal process in motion and should also define what you can expect them to do over the following weeks. Keep in contact with your solicitor as they will be your only means of assessing the status of the sale as it develops. Call into the office or telephone at least once a week to evaluate progress unless they contact you in the meantime. It is also worth communicating with your buyer once every couple of weeks to appraise the situation.

The legal process will ordinarily take between six and ten weeks to achieve completion. The most time consuming parts are often obtaining local searches and awaiting replies from buyer and seller. It is possible for a sale to conclude within days under the right circumstances, and with enthusiastic and competent solicitors acting on both sides . . . but this is rare! If you have followed the guidance given so far in this book you can be assured of the fastest possible completion, but anticipate it taking at least four weeks.

TO SUMMARISE

- Write the Heads of Terms details in block capitals to ensure they will be correctly interpreted by all parties and always add the phrase 'Subject to Contract' to the top of each page to protect yourself.

- Double-check that the information obtained is accurate and that names are spelled precisely.

- Send a copy of the details to the buyer for approval before issuing them to solicitors.

- Keep in regular contact with your solicitor and with the buyer to assess how the sale is proceeding.

13

If No Offer is Received

During the peak selling months of spring, summer and early autumn, and having followed the advice contained in this book, you can anticipate at least one offer being received within the first ten weeks of launching your property on the market. In the unlikely event that none is found you need to investigate the possible reasons and adjust or diversify your approach accordingly.

REVISING YOUR MARKETING STRATEGY

Have you achieved an abundance of viewings?
The primary objective of marketing your home was to generate a high volume of viewings within the first few weeks. If the strategies you employed failed to produce 20 appointments you should consider repeating the process, adding one or two alternative advertising methods to the plan. Manufacturing a high capacity of viewings is pivotal to success. The more bookings you can procure the more likely it is that an offer will be achieved. Before you embark on a major new publicity campaign, try moving the 'for sale' board to a new location – sometimes even the simplest action can bring about the desired result!

Is the price set too high?
Things change rapidly in the residential sales market and you must keep a close eye on what is happening to property prices both locally and nationally, otherwise your once accurate and competitive valuation can appear excessive and discouraging to buyers. Repeat the process outlined in Chapter 4 and assess the precision of your

original calculation set against a changing economic climate or/and an increasingly competitive local situation.

Estate agent's secret
Estate agents know that although reducing the price is often seen by vendors as the first and easiest option to attract viewers, it is rarely the most effective. There are often other discouraging elements involved and these should be tackled as a matter of priority. Instead of reducing the price, spend the sum on making improvements to the property if this is appropriate.

Consider what people have said

If five out of ten viewers have been honest enough to tell you that the kitchen design is out-of-date and a major reason why they have not submitted an offer, you can be certain that the other five viewers thought the same but were not brave enough to speak out. The comments made by viewers will direct you to where the problem lies and, finance permitting, you would be wise to concentrate your efforts on improving these areas. Once any work has been undertaken make sure you go back to all prior viewers to inform them.

PROPERTIES THAT ARE DIFFICULT TO SELL

A property in serious disrepair

Although you may have devalued the property appropriately, set against local competition, a home that is in need of major work is likely to discourage many potential buyers. Where it is impractical to have the repairs conducted, you will need to target advertising to those involved in the investment property market. These will ordinarily include first-time buyers, builders, private sector landlords and other developers who will see your home for the potential it has rather than the condition it may be in.

Ex-council homes and difficult estates

Your home may be a palace but if it is located in a poor area or amidst run-down neighbouring property it could prove difficult to sell. Local authority estates now comprise a mixture of privately owned and existing council owned accommodation and, whilst many are being gradually improved, there remains a number of significant problems associated with such estates. The issues often include:

- petty vandalism and litter

- poor landscaping and a lack of recreational space

- high levels of car-crime and burglary

- the perceived threat of assault or harassment from youths

- noisy neighbours

- low community spirit

- a lack of pride in the environment and poor respect for others.

Selling a property on estates such as these may often seem like an uphill struggle – but it is not insurmountable. Attention needs to be given to improving the area. Contact the local authority to find out if there is a residents' association that will give you support. Arrange a meeting with like-minded local people and organise a campaign targeted at specific objectives. If crime is the worst element – deal with this first before moving on to others. Contact the local police for advice on how to start a Neighbourhood Watch Scheme or see if the council will consider a scheme to improve street-lighting or the installation of a CCTV system.

The most damaging emotions of people on poor estates are feelings of isolation, apathy and low morale. Even the smallest of initiatives to create a sense of community can have a snowball effect that will lead to greater things. Look at ways of kick-starting this change and, who knows, you may eventually find you don't want to move at all. For those that do, improvements to the neighbourhood will gradually lead to individual properties becoming more attractive to a wider section of the community, prices will rise and a sale will be achieved.

Discrimination due to historical problems

Where an area is renowned for having had problems such as subsidence from coal-mining, pollution from industrial sites, and more recently flooding from nearby rivers, there is always going to be prejudice against buying such property even though the original cause may have been rectified or any danger from it eliminated.

Whilst it may be impossible to persuade some buyers that your property is safe, evidence of it can be convincing for others, so be certain to procure a report from the appropriate professional confirming the structural safety of your home and the land on which it is sited. Whilst it would not be prudent to present this to all potential buyers it will hopefully reassure anyone who specifically asks about such problems.

POSTPONING UNTIL THE MARKET CHANGES

Sometimes the answer is to *do nothing*! The residential property market occasionally falls into depression when prices tumble at the same pace as demand (rather than prices falling while properties become high in demand). This phase tends to occur when there is a national or world recession.

There is very little you can do in these circumstances but ride out the storm and wait until the economy improves, prices rise, demand outstrips supply, and the property market becomes buoyant again. During this void period you should take your 'for sale' board down and cease all advertising otherwise your home will stagnate in the eyes of would-be purchasers and particularly those in your neighbourhood.

ALTERNATIVES TO TRADITIONAL SELLING

Have you thought about property auctions?

Auctions are not for the faint-hearted but they are
sometimes a viable alternative to traditional selling
methods. The price the property sells at is self-adjusting
since it will largely depend on the number of people
attending who are keen to buy your home – and the
amount they are prepared to pay for it. A reserve price is
usually fixed so there is no danger of selling below a level
you are not prepared to accept. The advantages of selling
by auction are:

- It is quick . . . once the hammer falls the property is
  usually sold.

- A successful bidder must leave a secured deposit of
  around 10% of the selling price before leaving the
  auction room.

- If the bidder later withdraws they must pay
  compensation to the seller.

- Selling by auction is generally as cost-effective as
  selling through an estate agent.

The disadvantages include:

- If a property fails to achieve its reserve price there are
  still charges to pay to the auction-room for their
  services.

- People go to auctions to get a bargain – as a result your
  property may not sell for as high a price as otherwise it
  might using traditional methods.

- Much of the legal work needs to be undertaken before
  the auction takes place and sellers are advised to have
  their solicitor in attendance on the day – this can be
  costly, particularly if the property fails to sell.

The 'open-house' strategy

This method is a bit of a gamble and it doesn't always produce the desired results. It is nonetheless worthy of consideration because when it does succeed the effect produced is nothing short of remarkable. The idea is to create a spectacular advertising campaign which will introduce the property to the market – making it clear that viewing will only be conducted on one particular day and offers will be invited at the same time.

For this to work you should expect your home to be deluged with viewers, hence the term 'open house'. If the right number of interested viewers attend there can be a frenzy of offers received and, where two or three are keen to acquire the property, the asking price and more can be achieved. The success of this technique is to instil a sense of urgency amongst the buyers that forces them to make a quick and committed decision. This is based on the fact that they are looking at the property together with their competitors and any delay in securing a deal may cause them to lose the opportunity.

The danger, however, is that a large amount of capital can be expended on an advertising campaign which may fail on the day if only a handful of viewers turn up.

TO SUMMARISE

- Assess whether sufficient viewers have been attracted to achieve an offer and, if not, revise your advertising and check the validity of the selling price before re-launching your property on the market.

- Review the comments that viewers have made to identify problem areas on which you can concentrate your efforts.

- Procure help from like-minded neighbours, the police and the local authority to improve a deprived or problematic estate.

- If traditional selling methods have failed, try alternatives or remove the property from sale until the economic climate improves.

14

The Top Ten Selling and Moving Tips

1. DEALING WITH A BROKEN CHAIN

The biggest fear of most sellers and buyers is a chain that collapses en route to completion. It can be devastating, but the involved parties frequently give up all too easily without looking for a possible solution.

Quite often the problem lies at the start of the chain where a first-time buyer cannot raise enough additional funds to make the purchase. The sum involved is often below £1,000. In such circumstances ask your solicitor to investigate the chain and, if possible, seek an agreement from all others involved to collectively finance the first-time buyer's deficit – an outlay of just a couple of hundred pounds each could secure your sale and all other transactions involved.

2. VIEWING YOUR HOME AS OTHERS SEE IT

When analysing your home before and after making improvements, take photographs and examine them in a mirror. This will help you avoid the problems associated with familiarity as the resulting images will appear alien to you and, as a result, you will be able to view your home as others see it.

3. MAINTAINING SECURITY

Research from insurance companies shows that burglars are 50% more likely to strike while people are moving house! Routine security measures can easily be overlooked in the chaos. Be certain to inform your insurers and check the cover afforded under any existing policies. Employ a reputable removal firm and use their insurance as this will give them a vested interest in taking care of your possessions. Always change locks to doors and windows as soon as you move into your new home.

4. PLANNING AHEAD WHEN TAKING GARDEN PLANTS

Transplant any favourite plants and shrubs into pots at the appropriate time of the year so that you won't have to leave them behind should a sale be achieved when the soil is frozen solid.

5. TAKING METER READINGS

Always take the time to obtain your own meter readings for water, gas and electricity for the property you are selling and any property you are buying, then pass these on to the appropriate companies. If you don't you may find that you become liable for part of the prior owner's bill if they also failed to take readings.

6. AVOIDING DELAYS ON MOVING DAY

Arrange ahead of the completion date who will hold the keys once you have vacated the property. This is normally the estate agent but an arrangement can be made with your solicitor or with the buyer's solicitor. There is nothing to prevent you handing them over personally, but are you sure you want to wait around at your old home on the day of moving should they be delayed?

7. ASKING FOR A REDUCTION

In the unlikely event that you employ an estate agent to sell your property at some stage in the future, always ask for a reduction in the normal fees they charge. Most agents will be prepared to lower the percentage a little, or they may even offer a fixed fee to secure your custom. If there are several agents operating in your town explain to each that you are visiting the others to secure the best deal.

8. SAVING ON REMOVAL FEES

Dispose of all unwanted or unnecessary possessions before you move rather than taking them with you and then having to sort them out in your new home. This will save space in the removal van and may even reduce the number of trips needed, resulting in a reduction in the time and cost of moving.

9. AVOIDING HIGH RENTS

Be certain to meet the completion date proposed by your purchaser. If it seems increasingly unlikely that the dates for your sale and any new purchase will coincide exactly, consider temporarily moving in with friends or relatives and storing your furnishings instead of renting. Many landlords will only let property for a minimum six month term and where shorter periods are agreed it is often at the expense of an increased monthly premium.

10. PUTTING YOUR MOBILE PHONE TO GOOD USE

If you have a mobile telephone make sure that the battery is fully charged before your vacating day and give the number to your solicitor, the buyer and their solicitor, and to your removal firm. By doing this you can safely arrange for any landline to be disconnected in advance, preventing the new owners using the phone at your expense should they move in before disconnection takes place.

AND FINALLY . . .

As you progress through your sale, keep notes about anything and everything you learn from the experience. Attach them to this book for future reference so that when you decide to relocate again you will be even more prepared than you are now.

Index